BUG
TALES

**The 99 most hilarious, outrageous and touching tributes
ever compiled about the car that became a cultural icon**

Paul Klebahn • Gabriella Jacobs

D0112060

Oval Window

Press

Library of Congress Catalog Number
99-093047
Standard Address Number
299-8491
International Standard Book Number
0-9669474-0-1

Cover Design and Illustrations: Randy Rider
Select Photography: Jerome Veih
Layout: Bob Gleason and Brent Stewart

1 2 3 4 5 - 03 02 01 00 99

TABLE OF CONTENTS

CHAPTER ONE
GETTIN' BITTEN
First encounters
1

CHAPTER TWO
PARTS & SOUL
Bugs that left a lasting impression
37

CHAPTER THREE
HOW I GOT LOST ON THE ROAD LESS TRAVELED
THEN FOUND INSTANT KARMA ON I-96
Bug tales of the road
73

CHAPTER FOUR
A WING AND A SPARE
Breakdowns, fixes, and making it home
99

CHAPTER FIVE
CUPID HAS THE KEY
Bug tales of love
131

CHAPTER SIX
I SWEAR I'LL TURN THIS CAR AROUND...
Bug tales of family and children
149

CHAPTER SEVEN
WILD THINGS AND DOOR DINGS
Bug tales of animals and intrigue
183

CHAPTER EIGHT
NOW PLAYING
Bug tales of the playful and bizarre
205

ACKNOWLEDGMENTS

The origin of this book can be traced to my parents, Ray and Dorothy Klebahn. They have provided incalculable assistance. Special appreciation also goes to my wife, Gretchen, who endured many lonely evenings and weekends while this book took shape.

"Bug Tales" also required the cooperation and support of:

Mark Schlachter, owner of Metalkraft Coachwerkes and the friend who taught me as a teenager how VWs were the coolest cars on earth;

Peter Baden, a long-time friend who devoted countless hours to creating and maintaining the "Bug Tales" web site. Without him, this project would have been much more difficult;

The management and staff of Software Packaging Associates Inc., whose enthusiasm and assistance were vital;

Hans Jansen, for the generous use of his showroom-condition 1964 sunroof Beetle for our cover photo;

Dan Ouellette, for including the "Bug Tales" tale in "The Volkswagen Bug Book: A Celebration of Beetle Culture in America" (1999, Angel City Press, ISBN 1883318009);

Wally Pleasant, songwriter and performer, who wholeheartedly introduced "Bug Tales" to his audiences;

The numerous VW clubs, and members of the media, who publicized this project worldwide to help us find contributors;

And finally, the hundreds of wonderful people who shared their stories and photos with us, so we could share them with you.

Thank you all,

Paul Klebahn

PREFACE

Despite what you might expect, "Bug Tales" is not an automotive book in the traditional sense. Nor is it a Volkswagen history book. And it's not a repair manual.

"Bug Tales" concentrates on the human side of the VW experience. It demonstrates how these cars puttered their ways into the hearts and memories of millions. What they lacked in heat they made up for in warmth. Slowly, steadily, they became more than just a car to many people, they became a companion. Often, they even became a family member — the kind you can swear at but still love.

These "family members" accompanied our contributors throughout both the big and inconsequential parts of their lives. They were there when love bloomed, kids screamed, parts broke and animals intruded. As the backdrop to all those kinds of experiences these cars became a global icon.

So whether you owned a VW, knew someone who did, or simply recognize them on the road, you'll identify with the experiences portrayed in "Bug Tales." Enjoy the ride.

INTRODUCTION

Some of my earliest memories involve a VW. Specifically a red 1961 Bug with white leatherette interior which was my parents' only means of transportation at the time of my birth in 1964.

My accountant father took delivery of his new Bug in early '62. As conservative as he was, he couldn't stand to buy the VW stripped. He splurged for the optional back-up light. Soon after my arrival the back seat was removed and replaced with a makeshift playpen. As I recall, this was a particularly memorable feature during evasive traffic maneuvers. Today this probably accounts for my near-perfect impersonation of a pinball. Fortunately for my parents, this was the Sixties and the statute of limitations for child safety seat laws have long passed.

Sadly, I only knew this Bug for a short time. Even though I was an only child, my parents decided that a bigger car would be more desirable. The beloved Bug was traded in for a Dodge Coronet, but it was too late. I was bitten.

For about the next 10 years my only VWs were of the Matchbox variety, but my fascination for them never faded. Approaching driving age and living some distance away from high school it became apparent that the need for some basic transportation was in order. My father and I decided to go hunting for a used VW. We found and bought a faded black '74 Super Beetle that needed TLC. This car fit both of our visions, just not for the same reason. He saw a spartan economy car whereas I saw a blank canvas.

It didn't take long before this '74 was completely customized in the style of the day and winning trophies at regional shows. With Porsche wheels, etched glass, and custom paint one thing was certain — it no longer was basic transportation. While owning my custom Super Beetle, I also

bought and sold a number of other VWs including Karmann
Ghias and buses. There was nothing that could tear me away
from my fascination.

Well, maybe one thing. In my junior year of college I met
and fell in love with a beautiful girl named Gretchen. We were
married a year later. Now facing mortgage payments and trying
to make ends meet, we made a decision. We had to sell a car.
The '74 Super Beetle was in pieces going through yet another
customizing metamorphosis and we needed our daily
drive-to-work cars. We sold my teenage pride and joy "as is".
Thinking back on that sale still hurts. I guess it was a rite of
passage that I had to endure.

Although she never experienced a Beetle growing up,
Gretchen had also become fascinated. I guess my enthusiasm
was infectious. On a 1990 trip to Mexico, where original
Beetles are still made, she even insisted on renting a brand new
one. It was the highlight our trip and the source of a story or
two. It also stirred some strong feelings in me. As I thought
back through my life, I realized that some of my most vivid
memories, both good and bad somehow involve a VW. It was as
if there was always one around at important times. Learning to
drive, friends I've had, friends I've lost, falling in love and
growing up, a VW was always there as a constant companion.

Being a professional in sales for the last decade, I've come
in contact with a lot of people from CEOs on down the line.
Early on I discovered that I was not so unique. Sooner or later
as I'd get to know people the subject of VWs would inevitably
come up. No matter their profession or station in life, nearly
everyone has a VW memory whether they've owned one or not.
This car has truly made an impact.

Not long after this revelation, I began casually collecting
VW stories from people I knew as more less a hobby. I always
figured someday I'd do a book. Years went by and I quickly
tired of hearing myself say "Someday...." If I was going to do

this thing right I needed a partner. But who? Well duh!, who else? Not only did I marry a girl who was beautiful, but one who came with a sister who was a professional newspaper journalist and editor. It didn't hurt that she had owned a VW in the early '80s. It also didn't hurt that she owed me a BIG favor for helping her move in an ice storm some years before. For whatever reason the proposition/guilt trip worked. She accepted. Gabriella Jacobs became my partner and the Bug Tales project was begun.

Both of us have been constantly amused and touched by the hundreds of stories we received. Our contributors have been so enthusiastic that they've networked the "Bug Tales" tale around the world. For this we thank them and hope they enjoy what's been produced as a result.

CHAPTER ONE

GETTIN' BITTEN

First encounters

WON OVER

I remember when I first became aware of the Volkswagen. It was 1957. That ugly little car you began to see around town had a name. It was a Volkswagen, or VW for short. I didn't know much more than that, but who cared? At least you could identify it. I was newly married and driving a neat little British sports car.

Midway through '57 my wife, Lee, and I happened to be visiting another newly married couple. The gal was an old high school friend of Lee. Her husband just landed a job selling the Volkswagen at a new dealership. At the time he was driving a '56 VW sunroof sedan. I had a chance to look the car over at close range.

"Hmm. It was nicely made. The fit and finish were rather well done," I thought. And it had an air-cooled motor, in the rear, no less. That was radical. I had never seen a rear-engine car. But who would want something so ugly?

A year went by when my best friend paid a visit and told me he had ordered a VW. They didn't call them "Beetles" or "Bugs" yet. I was really surprised. He told me his reasoning. He did some research and found that they were a great little car.

The only problem, he lamented, was that he would have to wait anywhere from nine months to a year for delivery.

"You're kidding? A year?" He explained that the supply was limited and the demand was great. You put down a $100 deposit, picked out your color and model; sedan, sunroof or convertible, then waited for your dealer to call.

Several weeks later I was browsing the magazine rack at our local drug store and came across a small magazine entitled *Foreign Car Guide*. It had lots of stuff in there about Volkswagens so I bought a copy. I didn't realize it at the time but I was becoming hooked.

The more I read about the car, the more I became intrigued.

I even stopped at a then-new VW dealer and picked up some literature and took another look at the one and only showroom floor model. It was a new, '58 model, the salesman told me. He proceeded to tell me about all the improvements that had been made. A new, larger, rear window, larger windshield, new dashboard, directional lights, etc. The car looked nice. It actually looked nice. Not ugly. Nice.

I bought more issues of *Foreign Car Guide* and began to study the VW. That fall, Shell took delivery of his new VW. A medium blue one.

"But I thought you told me you ordered a black one," I said.

"I did. But they called me and said that my car had come in, a very sharp blue one."

"What did you say?"

"I said I ordered a black one. They said that yes, but what they had was a blue one. If I wanted to wait for the black one they'd keep my name on the list until one became available. They didn't know when that would be so I took the blue one."

"It does look sharp," I told him. But the black would have been my choice. A black VW was the car to have. Black with a red interior. Yeah!

In the spring of '59 I was hit head-on by a drunk driver. By today's standards my British car would have been totaled.

I went down to the local VW dealer, gave him $100 and placed my order for a black sedan with red interior. There was still a nine- or ten-month wait. In the meantime, I picked up some literature and went home to drool over the catalog. By now I was hooked. Volkswagens were really beautiful.

One day I was on my way home from an out-of-town business trip. I passed a used car lot. There in the front line sat five brand new VWs. I stopped to take a closer look.

I couldn't believe my eyes. The salesman told me that they were European model Volkswagens and had been converted to meet the U.S. vehicle standards.

I took a close look. They sure were different.

First of all, the dead giveaway was the lack of over-rider bumpers. These had a single blade with two small bumper guards. There were turn signal lights on the front fenders, like the ones at the dealer. But in addition to these there were signal sticks (semaphores) in the door posts. Inside, the upholstery was cloth and the speedometer was in kilometers. The odometer read 150. The owner's manual was in German.

It smelled new. It was new. "How much?"

"$1,595," he told me.

Sold!

There were three blue and two beige ones — Kalihari Beige, they called it — on the lot. My friend had a blue one, so I bought a beige one. And I didn't have to wait 10 months.

In one issue of *Foreign Car Guide* was an explanation that European VWs were being brought into the U.S. by independent importers because of the built-up demand. They called them "Bootlegged Bugs" — the Bug nickname had begun to stick.

The '59 was a terrific car. It was a terrific time to be a VW owner. It was like joining a fraternity. You paid no dues and you didn't know all the members by name, but you did know them by sight. Everybody who owned a Bug belonged. And you looked out for each other. If you passed on the road you beeped your horn and waved. If you were pulled over on the side of the road another Bug would stop and offer assistance. It was great.

Sure, the heater was bad. But after a fresh snowfall you could go up to the shopping center parking lot, late at night, when everyone was gone, and do donuts until you got dizzy.

The Volkswagen became a part of our family. You overlooked the bad heater in the winter and the lack of a gas gauge.

Hell, it was an adventure to drive a VW. Many was the day when that ol' Bug would begin to cough as the gas in the tank got low. But you just reached down to turn the handle to the reserve position, like you'd done so many other times, only to find that you forgot to turn it back when you filled up last time. Then you got out of the car and pushed it to the gas station. The guys in the station didn't bat an eye. It happened a lot.

The '59 served us well, even after our firstborn came along. You could pack a playpen and car bed in the back seat, no problem. We have had several Bugs since that first one, but somehow I remember it better than the rest.

Don Narus

BEETLE BOMB

The time was in the late 1950s. The location was a NATO air base in southwest Europe. An airman and his crew were preparing for a scheduled flight to transfer back to the U.S. after a long tour. This particular airman had just found and purchased a great treasure of Europe. It was a new VW Beetle, with only the mileage that was required to take it from the dealership to the air base.

The airman didn't have a chance to enjoy this treasure prior to his transfer back to the States but he was a trained professional who thinks on his feet. The problem: how does one retain his investment and ownership of this classic means of transportation without additional red tape and hassle of paid transport back to the States? The solution: a talk with the pilot and crew who had become part of his extended family.

Uncle Sam's aircraft had been flown several times with payloads that were 10 times the full weight of a Volkswagen Beetle without incident. After setting contacts at the arrival base, the airman and his crew began prepping the aircraft to carry the Bug inside its internal payload hold. How this was accomplished was not fully explained since most of the payloads of the Fifties were classified. I do know that security was high so the art of discretion was paramount in this scenario.

With the long-range capabilities of the aircraft a direct route was possible without refueling. The delivery looked to be almost complete. Upon the initial descent the aircrew inquired who was due to service the aircraft upon arrival. The reply was unexpected. Due to changes in the schedule the ground crew that was known to the aircrew and the airman had changed. Strangers would be there!

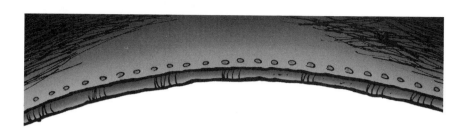

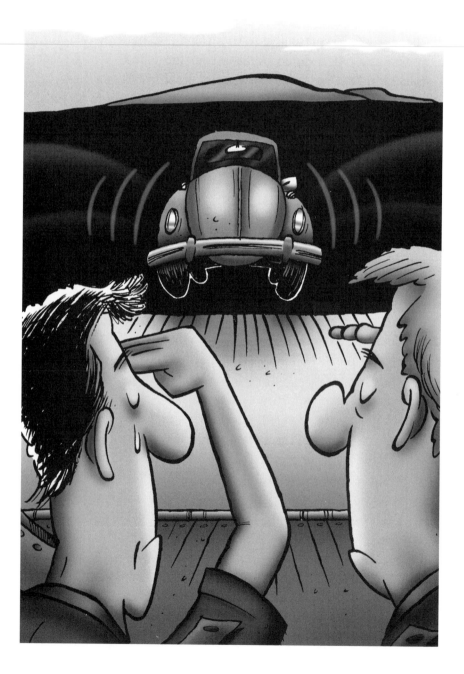

This caused an adjustment to the planned delivery of the Bug. The aircrew agreed that no explanation of the payload would be accepted by either the wing commander or base commander. Sadly, a decision was made to transfer the ownership of this particular piece of Air Force property to the Navy's jurisdiction — the Atlantic Ocean.

As the plane descended the payload was released. The airman said goodbye to his Beetle as it plunged. From that altitude, it didn't float for long. Now it's sunken treasure.

As told by Ron R.

BEEN THERE, DRIVEN THAT

Ever wonder how many cars you've driven, in total, since that very first time behind the wheel? This may sound like a strange query, unless you're as unabashedly crazed about cars as I've always been. Case in point: From age 10 to about 25 (when I lost count), I knew the year, make, model, color, engine size, horsepower, and a bunch of other minutiae about every car I'd ever driven. I knew all that because I'd written the details of each new driving encounter in a special notebook, a tome more dear to me in my pre-legal driving years than anyone could imagine. Yes, I was a bit twisted. But it's tough being a car guy who's too young to get a license.

That journal began one incredible windfall day when my Dad suggested I back his indigo blue 1960 Beetle out of the garage. I'd had years of car steering experience from atop Dad's lap (great big V-8 machines such as my Mom's '64 and '67 Cadillacs and my Grandad's '62 Buick Electra 225), but nothing like the angst-riddled thrill of operating all three pedals of a 34-horsepower V-Dub. When it was over, I was in a bit of a daze. Wow, I'd really driven a car. Sure, only for about 25 feet, but I'd done it, alone, and hadn't hit anything in the process. To say it was a more exciting moment for me than every Christmas and birthday put together would be an understatement. I bought the notebook that afternoon to record my experience and doubtless impress my 10-year-old cronies.

Additional driving stints were few and far between, but by age 13, I'd shoed in five more cars. Immediately, I began bringing *Motor Trend* and other car mags to school, transcribing test data charts in class instead of math equations. Mad Car Disease had become chronic.

Not surprisingly, I also pestered my Dad each weekend to take me to another new-car dealer to look at some machine I thought he couldn't live without owning — sensible family cars like the Datsun 240Z, Corvette 454 convertible, or Lamborghini Miura. Dad would always initially say *no*, but most of the time he relented enough to let me run in and collect sales brochures that I'd cut apart and tape to my bedroom walls. On very rare occasions I could coerce him into taking a test drive and sometimes, on quiet side streets he'd let me pilot for a few blocks. By the time I got my driver's license, I'd driven a heady 18 cars.

Each writer for my magazine, *Motor Trend,* drives an amazing number of new vehicles each year. In addition to the 300 or so we road test collectively are probably another 300 we'll sample at press introductions. Based on my 17 years in the car mag biz, I've calculated I would now have something like 3,000 entries on my "been there, driven that" list. However, by 1983 I was going to so many new-car intros I simply lost count — which means my driving experiences with dream cars such as the Porsche 959, Cobra 427, and (finally!) a Lamborghini Miura had best not fade from my overtaxed memory.

I came across that tired old notebook the other day while cleaning the garage, The early pencil writings were fading and the paper was yellowed, but it was almost as much of a joy to read back through those first entries as it was to create them. Those were special times with my Dad that I'll never forget. It all started with his VW and that old notebook.

So, if you have any budding young car enthusiasts in your family, I know a great gift for them.

C. Van Tune
Editor of Motor Trend *magazine*

SAVED BY THE BUG

Although I have never owned a Bug, there is that little voice deep within that secretly longs for one. The voice is hard to understand, since I have been a passenger only once.

It was the summer of 1977 and I was all of 10 years old. I took my bicycle out for a spin, like I did every Saturday. On this particular day, I had a purpose. The track which I had built with friends over the course of years was destined to become a housing tract. I thought this would be the last day I would be allowed to ride on this property that had been "mine" for years.

I crossed the starting line, full of the energy possessed only by 10-year-olds, and blasted around the first corner. I knew I had to have my speed up to get to the top of the hill. It was something I had done hundreds of times before, and I was saddened that this would be my last ride. With the speed I had picked up, I knew I could do a jump on the top of the hill, something only the biggest kids could have even thought of. This was the day I had been waiting for my entire life. I was bulletproof. I was the world's greatest stunt man. I was invincible. I was airborne! I howled with pleasure as I glided over the crest.

Suddenly I realized the other half of the hill, my landing area, had been taken away by trespassers — huge, earth moving machines. My howl of pleasure became a shriek of fear. Dead ahead was a bulldozer. I landed right smack into the back of it, smashing my bike, as well as my face, against it. I was bleeding. I thought I was dying but I could still see light when I closed my left eye.

I rode the bent and twisted wreck of a bike back home, and asked my father if we had any Band-Aids. The pain had subsided on the ride, or wobble, home. He looked at me, took three steps back, then charged me. He threw me under his arm

like a living football, running for the end-zone, which in this
case was the blue Bug that belonged to Ron, the neighborhood
hippie.

Ron was giving the Bug its weekly wash. Dad threw me in
the passenger's seat, jumped into the driver's seat, fired the Bug
and took off speeding down the road. (In a 10-year-old's world,
a Bug could go off speeding down a road.) I remember Ron
looking at us very confused as we sped off. I waved goodbye as
the hose filled his shoes with water.

I received four stitches to my eyelid that day, and got my
first ride in the legendary Bug. At the time, I thought it was a
pretty fair tradeoff. Ron never really forgave us for treating his
pride and joy like a racing car, or for my bleeding on his white
interior.

Over the years, I made many friends in the new tract and the
scars of the bulldozer incident served as a point of interest in a
world of pretty faces for years. The bite of the Bug, however,
has remained strong in my heart. One day, I will own a Bug and
let the neighbor kid bleed in it. Someone has to keep the
nostalgia disease spreading.

William G. Van Der Woude

RED-FACED ABOUT FACE

We were very excited to be going to the dealer to get our brand new 1967 white Volkswagen Beetle. My husband drove it home and of course, many neighbors came to see it. After all, it did have an engine in the rear and the trunk under the hood.

My husband invited two of the men to take a little spin in his new car. Off they went to a nearby shopping center. He carefully pulled head-first up against the parking curb. The trio climbed out and made some quick purchases. When it was time for the return home everything seemed fine until my husband was ready to back out. No matter what he tried he couldn't get the novel little car to go into reverse. He'd had no trouble getting it to go forward on the way there. But now, in front of his cronies, the car was outsmarting him. He was stumped.

Suddenly the passengers got an inspiration. They climbed out and walked around to the front. After a quick consultation the men simply grasped the Bug by the bumper, picked up the front end and swivelled the car around 180 degrees. Voila! No reverse gear needed!

My husband was embarrassed and very anxious to get home and read the operating manual. That's when he learned that you had to push down on the gear shift to engage reverse. This was probably the first thing he taught our son and daughter when they learned to drive. And the last thing our neighbors would ever forget.

We loved that car and bought another one in 1972. By that time, we were Volkswagen veterans.

Suzanne Carnahan

TRANSPORTATION ORCHESTRATION

My 1966 red Beetle was found by my father (but paid for by me) in 1967 and lovingly embraced as (a) transportation and (b) my very first motor vehicle. It had nearly invisible tail lights and a heater that only began to work when you got where you were going. But it was nearly invincible.

It came to pass that my younger sister, Jo, and I shared a dwelling and it also came to pass that she needed transportation for her musical instrument — a full size, standing double bass. Jo devised a way to take out the back seat to make room for her bass. It worked, believe it or not. The story of all this lies in the fun we had after concerts when the "audience" would gather just to watch her get that huge thing into the Bug. Some didn't believe it could happen; others made sly comments about circus clowns emerging from a car. Anyway, it was fun to see the reactions. It was more fun knowing there wasn't much that Bug couldn't do.

Kristin Hansen

THE BUG THAT GOT BUSTED

When I was 16 years old and had just passed my test for a driver's license, my father gave me an electric orange, 1969 VW Bug. I was so excited!

The first thing we had to do was clean it up because it had belonged to a guy with a serious hygiene problem. When we finally got all the greasy dirt off the basket weave seats we realized they were white. My stepmother was worried that I had no spare tire, so we had to work really hard to open the trunk and once we did she about had a heart attack. The trunk had been packed full with homegrown marijuana drying. The previous owner had been such a serious entrepreneur he had screened in the entire trunk area so it would not be scattered. Needless to say, with sweeper in hand my stepmother started going crazy to get it all contained, because there were four curious teens standing guard.

The first thing that happened was my father took me to a shopping center approximately 15 or so miles from the house to instruct me on driving a standard shift. He said to me, "You do not need this fourth gear. Never take it out of third." So we drove around the parking lot for about 30 minutes until he approved of my technique. Then we started home. Being a good girl and also minding what my Daddy said (for fear of his wrath), I did as I was told and never took it out of third gear. I drove 55 to 60 miles and hour for about 20 minutes to stop at a stop sign to see my car go up in smoke.

Dad got out of his truck and demanded "What in the hell have you done?" I explained that I had done as instructed all the way home, third gear on a very mountainous highway. Then he started to go off and stopped and said, "Well, I thought you would be smart enough to know to use fourth gear on the highways." How would I know that? I had lived in the city all my life and drove an automatic.

After a couple months, Dad called me and said he was bringing my car. I could drive him back to the country and spend the weekend. It would be my first highway trip alone. When he got to town, I had to go show my girlfriend my new car. It was so cool, everyone wanted one, and I had a big ol' pumpkin.

I got to her house and she wanted us to go to check on her boyfriend at football practice. We pulled out of her driveway and at the end of her street was a grade. Being new to standard shift, the car kept dying, and I couldn't get up the hill. I had the car in gear and was giving it lots of gas. Then we start to move. We moved all right, backward right into a '62 Oldsmobile. I completely lost it. I had my car for only 20 minutes and smashed the rear right fender off. During the crash my 90-pound friend broke my passenger seat; now it lays down flat all the time.

I called my parents. As my Mom picked up the phone I heard my Dad in the background say something to the effect of "Oh, hell. She wrecked the damn thing." I hate when he is right. And from that day on all my friends fought over who got to ride in the back seat behind the driver because the famous concrete block held up my seat for another three years until it went to the big VW resting place.

Elizabeth Ditto Beam

DANCING THROUGH LIFE WITH CATHERINE

I was a senior in high school and still hadn't gotten my driver's license. One evening during Christmas break, I decided to get a Bug. A Bug would be easy to learn to drive, I thought.

I answered an ad in the paper for a real clean '66 Beetle. My Dad and I were instantly impressed. The Bug was very complete and had only three-week-old paint, too! A short test drive revealed little to complain about so a deal was struck.

The senior prom was fast approaching and I really wasn't in the mood to have my parents drive me again. Basically, I had four weeks to cram six months worth of driving experience into. And man, did I ever drive a lot. Any time my folks could come up with a reason to go somewhere, I was in the Bug and behind the wheel! I had a great time, learning the quirks and joys of my Beetle!

The four weeks quickly came and went and it was now the afternoon before senior prom. Of all the near scrapes I've had, this was probably the closest; having my driver's license test on the afternoon before prom at what was known as the toughest DMV in Silicon Valley! To compound things, we had forgotten some of the necessary paperwork and had to rush all the way home and back, hoping we could still get in before 5 p.m.

Amazingly, we made it back with just enough time for me to take the test. I was sweating bullets since I knew that the car liked to pop out of second if I eased off the gas while it was still in gear. I couldn't let that happen. After the test, I felt confident, but the DMV lady who had ridden along with me pointed out stuff I did wrong. I nodded, apologized, and faked my way through enough excuses. If I was sweating bullets earlier, I must have been shoving thermonuclear devices out my pores now! Had I failed? Was I going to be stuck having my parents drop me off at the prom while all my other friends were coming in their own cars?

"You passed. But barely," she emphasized, "With a 70." I danced like a lame quarterback after the lady had retreated to the safety of her cubicle inside. I was a legal driver and, moreover, I had freedom! No longer did I have to rely on my bike or on my parents to get me places.

Well, I learned more about driving that Beetle on that cold and rainy prom night. Important lessons like — not to drive in wet patent leather shoes (they slip right off the pedals; I wound up driving in socks the whole time) and to always carry a rag in the car to clear the windscreen. My date and I caravanned with another couple to a restaurant downtown, following his light blue '66 Beetle the whole way. It was cool.

I spent the next couple years restoring Catherine (as I later named her) and showing her off whenever I could. In September of 1996, at a car show in Campbell, California, all my efforts were rewarded when I won first place in my class. Sadly, just three months later Catherine was severely rear-ended by a drunk driver in a pickup truck. I was lucky enough to escape with only a sore neck, a charley-horse, and one small scratch on my wrist but Catherine was totaled. I don't remember much else about that night of that wreck. I don't really want to. But I will always remember Catherine: the best Bug I've ever owned.

Taylor Nelson

A MATCH MADE IN HEAVEN

We had been living in Germany for my job and had four kids. It became apparent that our 1962 Beetle was no longer enough. It was '68 and the newly redesigned VW buses with the sliding side door had just arrived at the dealership. This seemed to be the perfect vehicle for our growing family. We picked out a blue one and bought it for only $1,850 — only $400 more than we paid for the Bug in 1961. It turned out to be everything that we expected.

A year later when we were to come back to the U.S. we decided this would be the VW we would bring with us. We moved to Concord, California and used it as our everyday vehicle and makeshift camper for a number of years. In 1976, we decided we would like to go one step further with our camping hobby so we began looking for a used VW camper with the "pop top" to replace the '68 bus.

We learned about a '74 camper being sold by a college girl not far away. My wife and I made arrangements to see the vehicle later that same day. It was orange with orange and brown plaid interior and curtains. By the time we had arrived another couple was looking at it and just left for a test drive. The young lady selling it informed us that the other couple wanted to buy it and were going to go to the bank to secure a loan. Sensing our disappointment she said we could test drive it if we liked and she would call us if things didn't work out with the other couple. We took her up on her offer and it drove wonderfully. It was exactly what we had dreamed of. It had the full kitchen including sink, stove, refrigerator, fold-out beds and all those cabinets for storage.

Miraculously, the young lady called the next day to tell us the other couple's loan didn't go through. She invited us to come see the camper again, asking if we were still interested.

Before we left for another test drive, I told my wife that we'd have to come up with a figure to offer for the camper. She suggested that we each write a figure on a piece of paper. We'd say a little prayer about it and see what would happen. Seconds later we wrote our offers and traded papers. We were amazed to find that we had come up with exactly the same figures. We'd go $5,000 for the camper, we'd sell our '68 for $1,500 and get a loan for the balance of $3,500. At least we were in agreement.

The seller went with us on the test drive. It drove well...really well. Soon my wife and I would make our offer and hope for the best. On the way back, we asked the young lady why she was selling it. She replied that she really liked it, but it seemed like such a waste since she would never use it for camping. She went on to say she liked VWs and wished she could find a nice plain bus. "Really?" I said with the wheels of my mind turning. "Yeah", she replied, "I really want a blue one." Suddenly, a light went on in her mind. "Hey! What are you guys going to do with your old one?"

The next thing we knew we were in our old VW bus with this young lady at the wheel test driving it. She loved it and asked if we would take $1,500 for it and give her $3,500 for hers. Our jaws dropped in amazement. These were the exact same figures we had individually come up with. We knew divine intervention was at work. The young lady mistook our astonishment for an objection to the price and started frantically throwing out offers of $1,600, followed without a breath by $1,700. My wife and I exchanged glances and warmly said "No, the price is $1,500." We told her the story of how we prayed this would work out and we knew we had each found the right buyer for our VWs. It was a VW match made in heaven.

We put over 100,000 miles on that VW. We camped all over the country in it and finally sold it in 1991. Oh, do we miss it.

Dick Imhoff

CREAM PUFF

There's something about finding and refurbishing old air-cooled Volkswagens that really makes my adrenaline pump. Maybe that's why they call me the Old Beetle Finder.

I suppose it's like searching for the Holy Grail; once you're hooked on it, it never lets you go. Today was no exception. One of my informants, a young man who mows lawns, had reported a Beetle sighting less than a mile from my home in a Cincinnati suburb.

Knowing what to wear is almost as important as what to say during a visit with the original or second-generation owner of a Beetle. Folks who have owned VWs since the Fifties or Sixties usually treat their cars with a sense of reverence.

This particular Saturday morning I decided to wear a clean, white dress shirt without a tie, khaki twill trousers and a well-worn pair of white leather walking shoes for my visit. My source had told me that Ed and Jane were in their sixties, somewhat reclusive, extremely nice, but also rather conservative. It was important that I not appear overbearing or pushy. I carefully maneuvered our 1958 VW sedan up a sloping driveway and onto the property shortly before noon. The shiny black paint, silver chrome trim and wide whitewall tires on our '58 were always great conversation starters and helped break the ice. It also demonstrated my future intentions about how I might care for any Volkswagen someone sold me.

I immediately observed several people working in the yard adjoining an ageless, weather-beaten wood frame house. The two older persons were no doubt Ed and Jane. A younger, bearded man bore some resemblance to Ed so I assumed he might be a son.

Ed barely glanced in my direction before retrieving a portable oxygen tank and going toward the rear of the house. He evidently wasn't comfortable meeting strangers. Jane acknowledged my arrival with a friendly stare, but continued weeding a flower bed while the man I assumed to be their son disappeared among the trees with a self-propelled lawn mower whining at high speed.

I introduced myself to Jane and told her of my "Beetle finder" vocation. "It's not for sale," she told me, and added that it had belonged to her father.

"I'll treat your father's car like it's a part of my own family. Please look at the VW I'm driving. Doesn't that tell you something about how I care for these beautiful old cars? Trust me..."

The younger man, John, had finished his mowing. He took me to an open shed adjacent to a closed garage near the rear of the property.

The scene was exactly as my informant had described it. A 1965 pearl white sedan, dirty beyond belief. The wheels and bumpers were full of rust and partially buried in mud and leaves. The engine compartment was full of spider webs and the windows were covered with so much gunk it was almost impossible to see inside. John said it hadn't been driven for about four years.

I tried to convince John to sell it to me but he said his mother was very attached to it. She associated it with memories of her father, he said. "She often comes here and talks to him as though my grandfather was still sitting behind the steering wheel preparing to drive off somewhere."

We agreed I could check back a few months later, which I did. But that time, I learned from a neighbor that Jane had passed away. The neighbor let me use her phone to call Ed. He remembered me, but still was reluctant to sell the car.

The following spring a note on my calendar triggered a call to Ed's son, John. He might be more effective in persuading his father to set a higher priority for disposing of the poor, neglected Beetle. Sadly, I learned that Ed, too, had recently passed away. For a minute, I almost decided not to ever contact this family again. I was beginning to believe I was a bad luck omen for them.

Something prompted me to visit the house about a month later, if for no other reason than to reassure my old Beetle friend that he hadn't been completely forgotten.

The ground was overgrown with honeysuckle vines, evergreens and various grasses. All of the gardens were in terrible shape except for a few wildflowers.

I picked up a scraggly old broom someone had left leaning against the garage door and began brushing aside the debris and cobwebs which now almost completely covered the forlorn Beetle. "What can I possibly do to get you out of this hopeless mess, my old friend?" I said out loud.

"Take me home with you please. Take me home," a soft female voice whispered from somewhere behind me.

The sound of another human voice coming from among the ghost-like pines surrounding the creaking wood garage startled me, to say the least. I spun around to see a young woman standing scarcely 10 feet away. She told me she was Elaine, John's sister. She said she was there to inventory her parents' belongings. Then she invited me inside. She said she had owned the Bug, too. She was the third generation of her family to have possession of it.

Then she reached into a pile of papers on the kitchen table, extracted a small document and handed it to me. It was the title to the Bug.

"All you have to do is write me a check for some reasonable amount and the car is yours. John and I talked and we both want you to have it. We simply couldn't imagine anyone else who would take care of it the way you undoubtedly will. I do have one request, though."

She said her German grandfather, the original owner, had

purchased the Beetle in 1965. "It was his absolute pride and joy. He drove it everywhere until he was almost 90 years old. He was particularly fond of the German Oktoberfest celebration. As you know, the Cincinnati version has now grown in size to where it's second only to the original held in Munich every year."

I listened intently, but remained puzzled. "A wonderful story. But what's your request?

"Restore it completely," she said."Make it absolutely new again. Then promise me you'll drive it through the streets of Cincinnati during Oktoberfest so everyone can see our lovely little Beetle the way it looked over 30 years ago. You will make me, my mother, and my grandfather very happy if you do this one thing. You see, everyone must know about the magic Beetles that once roamed the world in such large numbers. Will you do it?"

"Elaine, you have my word," I said.

The next afternoon a flatbed trailer with a winch hauled the newly baptized "Cream Puff" out of the mud and leaves and into the sunlight for the first time in four years. I could almost swear one of the headlights winked at me and the trunk lid had a wide grin on it while it was gradually being pulled up onto the trailer.

True to Volkswagen form, Cream Puff roared to life after we installed a new battery, plugs and points and a condenser. It seemed like he had only been hibernating a few months instead of being left to a life of neglect. Next stop was a friend's restoration shop, then Oktoberfest.

Cream Puff will always be among the dozens of "celebrity" Volkswagens in our city's Oktoberfest. Look for it dressed in a new pearl white exterior, red vinyl interior and narrow whitewall radial. You might even get a wink from it if you wave.

W.W. Fitzpatrick

THE RED MENACE

The Volkswagen people have brought out a new car they say is a Beetle. Yeah, right. You betcha.

Anyone who knew a Beetle or Super Beetle back in the Sixties or Seventies knows this is impossible. There can be no Nineties Beetle or Y2K Beetle. The Beetle was a creature of its time. Its time is gone. It doesn't belong in the age of microchips and cellular phones. It had too much soul.

Even now, years after I last knew him, I think of the Red Menace more as a friend than as an automobile. Indeed, the word "automobile" seems too ... well, mechanical ... to describe him.

The Menace was a 1973 Volkswagen Super Beetle. In '77, when I was going through the pain of divorce, I turned the family car over to my ex and had to find a replacement — a cheap one — for myself. I found the Menace listed in the newspaper classifieds, and a friend drove me over to take a look.

The owner was a teacher who said he used the Menace only to drive back and forth to school. It may have been true. The Menace's red coat, his chrome headlight rims, door handles and bumpers were pristine and shiny, His interior was immaculate. His mileage was low. I bonded with him at first sight and didn't quibble much over price. The owner wanted $2,000 for him, I offered $1,500, we settled for $1,800. It was the bargain of my life.

I had never owned a VW before, and didn't know that most owners of Beetles and Super Beetles felt compelled to give names to their cars and refer to them as "him" or "her." I thought I was being original, calling my car the Red Menace and designating him a male.

But I wasn't just being cute. From the first, the Menace, unlike any other machine I had ever known, seemed to have an attitude. Despite his small size, his un-sleek shape and tiny, churning engine, he seemed cocky, even aggressive. He seemed to dare the drivers of bigger, fancier cars to treat him as inferior.

And he was the perfect companion for a broke, lonely, divorced guy. He would chum along almost forever on a tank — a small tank — of gas. He required little maintenance. And during the years I drove him, his little engine didn't require a single major repair.

His body, however, was another matter. Like many small, feisty guys, the Menace seemed to attract trouble.

During the Great New Year's Eve Ice Storm of 1978-79, for example, the Menace was sitting quietly in the driveway of my garage apartment and a tree fell on him. A guy with a chain saw had to uncover him. Miraculously, the Menace suffered only a small dent and a paint chip on his left front fender, too small to bother repairing. His first battle scar.

Later that winter, I parked the Menace on a street during a snowstorm, I returned to discover that some idiot had skidded into him, badly denting his left rear fender and bending his rear bumper out of shape. It now extended from the Menace's body like a huge hitchhiker's thumb.

The attacker, of course, left no note under the windshield wiper. No phone number. No offer to compensate me for the Menace's injuries. And I, being broke, carried only liability insurance. So these scars, too, remained.

The following spring, the newspaper where I was employed sent me out of town on an overnight assignment and I left the Menace in the company parking lot. I returned to discover that some idiot had backed his car into the Menace's left door, leaving a deep dent the size of a washtub. Again, no note under the windshield wiper.

Maybe a month later, the Menace and I were stopped at a red light and a car containing two young men pulled up beside us. "Hey!" one of them yelled at me. "We'll fix those dents for you real cheap!"

I told the young men to follow me and led them to my

driveway. They examined the Menace's wounds and offered to repair his body for $100. I hired them. They pulled some tools out of their trunk and went to work. They hammered out the dents in the fenders and filled the big dent in the door with that gray goop that body repair shops use. The young men told me they were from Michigan and were working their way to the Gulf Coast, paying their way by picking up repair jobs like mine.

They banged on the rear bumper, but couldn't get it back to its original shape. They fixed the thumb so that it didn't stick out so far, though, and knocked $15 off our agreed fee.

With the big splotch of gray goop on his left door, the Menace seemed more menacing than ever. He resembled an aging, gotch-eared tomcat or a veteran waterfront brawler. Driving him on the Dallas North Tollway was one of the cheap pleasures of my bleak life. The Cadillacs, the Mercedes Benzes, the BMWs fled his proximity like the saloon patrons in an old Western movie when the bad guy walks in. I felt like Jesse James, terrifying the snooty nabobs with my faithful sidekick, Red.

The following summer, I had custody of my sons, ages 8 and 5. We loaded up the Menace with everything I owned, including the only item of value, a new IBM Selectric typewriter that I had just purchased to write my new novel. We headed for Corpus Christi and Port Aransas for my boys' first experience of beaches, then west on Interstate 10 to spend the rest of the summer at my family home in Fort Davis. I would work on my book and my city-bred boys would enjoy a Tom Sawyer summer in the mountains.

All went well until we reached Fort Stockton, only 80 miles from our destination. While filling the Menace's gas tank, I noticed that a huge chunk of rubber was missing from a rear tire. The station attendant had no tires for sale and the only places that sold tires were closed. He put on the spare and assured me that the boys and I surely could make 80 measly miles without more trouble.

But halfway between Fort Stockton and Balmorhea, one of the loneliest 50-mile stretches of road in Texas, just as the sun was sinking behind the distant mountains, the other rear tire blew out.

I never felt such helpless despair. "Oh, my God," I thought, "These little boys are going to have to spend the night in this tiny overcrowded car. Out here in the desert. And we have nothing to eat."

At that moment, I heard a chugging in the distance. Coming over the horizon like a miracle was an ancient Mercury, as dented and scarred as the Menace himself. I waved. The Mercury pulled over and stopped.

In the front seat sat two young cowboys with turkey feathers in their hatbands. They said they were headed to El Paso, and thence home to Mexico. In the back seat were two Anglo hippies. They were hitchhiking from Fort Lauderdale to Los Angeles. All four were smoking pot and were high as kites.

I was very nervous. But as it turned out, we couldn't have been rescued by nicer fellows. They gave us a ride to a service station in Balmorhea. They waited while I phoned to ask my mother if she could come pick us up. Our rescuers chugged away, with our everlasting gratitude. The gas station owner put four tires on the Menace the next day.

During his night in the desert, anyone could have stopped, broken him and stolen my new typewriter and all our belongings. But no one did. They were afraid, I think. Of Red Menace.

Later that summer, a guy in Marfa gave him a bright, new, red paint job, cheap. And we lived happily ever after. Until that midnight when the Menace and I got into trouble with the Highland Park cops and I wound up in jail.

But that story is better left untold.

Bryan Woolley
(Used with permission of The Dallas Morning News*)*

THE BALLAD OF HOOTER AND GROOVEY

My wife, Donna, has wanted a "hippie bus" (what others called simply a VW bus) since she was 16 years old. Last year I got her one: a 1971 that I found in a local tow yard. We bought it for a mere $175 — that included having it brought to our house on a flatbed truck, as there was no key, the motor was not running, and many other small such items. But it was ours. Donna quickly named it "Hooter".

That next day was beautiful and sunny so we got the dogs in the bus and went to the beach (never leaving the driveway). Later my neighbor Dave, a former auto mechanic, helped me haul Hooter up the hill to his house to see what we had gotten into.

After installing a new battery, starter, battery cables, new ignition key, and a few other odds and ends, we put some gas in, turned the key and Hooter was reincarnated. We all jumped around and danced. He lives!

There was one hitch, though. Once I got a real good look at the undercarriage I found too many things to replace to make it safe on the road. Hooter's road trips were destined to remain imaginary.

Donna told a friend of ours on the sheriff department about Hooter, and he told her about an abandoned 1974 VW bus that he had ordered towed a few months earlier. The good news is we located it. The bad news is the motor was in the bus — I mean inside where the people sit — all in pieces. Donna went to work wheeling and dealing. When the dust settled we owned a second VW bus for a paltry sum of $300, which included the tow yard owner bringing it to our house on a flatbed truck. Again no key, battery, battery cables or starter. The body was in great shape but the engine was DOA. Hooter's new companion quickly had a name, however: "Groovey."

We found an engine for Groovey in yet another abandoned bus. While cleaning it off I saw a rebuild tag from Canada. I went back to the tow yard where we got the engine and went through the remaining body for any paperwork on the rebuild. All I found was an old proof of insurance card with a lady's name and address on it. I went home and wrote to her of our tale of woe. I asked if she might have owned the bus when the engine was rebuilt and if so, did she happen to remember anything about it. Any "family history" would be useful.

I waited, hoping but not expecting to ever hear from her. Two weeks later I got a letter from her telling me yes, she had owned the bus. She had called it "Sylvia" and indeed, the engine was rebuilt. We had a match! Sylvia was a suitable donor for Groovey's part transplant!

Groovey's operation hasn't occurred yet due to all the ice and snow. But that hasn't stopped us and our dogs from taking many trips all over the country in him (never leaving the driveway). A relative christened both Hooter and Groovey by spraying patchouli oil in them. He also has given us some Jerry Garcia decals for the windows. A friend gave us a "flower power" sticker from a collectible shop San Francisco. The buses are far out now, man! Wave when we go by!

Donna and Rick Bayles

THE TREASURE BUS

A few years ago, my wife Barb and I took the kids away to the family cottage in our 1971 VW pop-top camper. While visiting Big Rapids, home of Ferris State University, we spotted homemade signs on every storefront reading "Estate Sale. Household Items. Sporting Goods. Tools. VW minivan."

Being a vintage VW fanatic, I was drawn like a magnet to the given address. I visualized every VW collector's dream: a sealing wax red and ivory '59 sunroof deluxe bus with a complete interior, no rust, and a smooth-running motor. In reality, it turned out to be a white rusted and rotted '67 priced at $500. It featured a unique homemade wood camper interior with several storage cabinets. Also included were some Beetle seats and an extra motor. The estate sale ringleader assured me that the bus would run but not idle. I assessed the motor and a quick half-turn of the adjustment screw had it idling placidly.

Thinking I could part this mess out for a small fortune, I offered $100 to "get the monkey off their backs." A family conference ensued with much mumbling and hissing. We had a deal! After I removed the ghastly foam rubber mattress from the rear and scanned the cab for clues, I found a service logbook documenting everything from delivery in March of 1967 through a transmission fluid change in June of 1993. Every valve adjustment, oil change and brake shoe was noted in painstaking accuracy with dates and recorded mileage. The odometer admitted to 71K on its second spin.

"It seems OK mechanically," I deadpanned to the family point person, a scowling brunette about my age.

"My stepfather related to things, not people!" she sneered, handing me the endorsed, original "Owner A" title.

Within 15 minutes I had checked the oil and fan belt, topped off the fuel tank and inflated a low tire. In no time we were cruising a steady 65 down U.S. 131. The thing ran like a train. Fuming, Barb had to break 70 mph in our camper just to keep up.

Back at the cottage I began the arduous task of body rust assessment and an inventory of contents left behind by the man who "related to things" and not people. In addition to all the rust, we found two ladies diamond rings, a mountain of costume jewelry, two 14-karat gold ladies dress watches, some very old silver dollars and several assorted foreign coins. We also found several mens watches, lots of funky sunglasses, some tools, mosquito netting for two, some camping gear and some slinky black lingerie complete with garter belts. Literature consisted of original owners and service manuals, county maps with trout streams marked with colored pencils, and the aforementioned service logbook. What would a detective — or psychiatrist — make of these clues?

Later that year my six-year-old son Hal and I painted the bus in a free-form Sixties motif, using every spray can of Krylon, Rust-O-Leum and barbecue paint I could find in the basement. We drive it occasionally to the delight of my children and wincing of my neighbors. Maybe its previous owner couldn't relate to people. But the bus sure does.

Keith Price
(Portions have previously appeared in the NEATO *and* MVVC *newsletters)*

COMMENCEMENT

I always wanted a VW Bug for my very own. My entire family at some point in their lives owned a vintage air-cooled VW. Now it was my turn to have my first car. My aunt was the only person I knew in the family who still had their original VW.

I begged her for years to eventually sell that shiny yellow '74 Super Beetle to me. She casually blew me off every time. The power was in her hands and all I could do was wait.

When I graduated from high school my aunt sent me a congratulatory card. It was full of the regular sentiment, but off to the side was a simple little drawing of a VW Bug. She was going to help me get the car! I nearly hit the roof with glee!

There was one hitch. My aunt lives in Houston and I lived on a military base in the sticks of Missouri. A trip to Texas was not in the near future. I restlessly spent the first semester of college without that great car.

Christmas of 1989 was the pickup date. The entire family gathered in Houston. My aunt was going to sign over the car to me FINALLY.

My father and I sat at the table with her as she pored over all the paperwork she had meticulously kept all those years. I tried to be patient but was anxious to just get the deal done and go. Then I noticed tears well up in her eyes as she remembered the '74's first tune-up and oil change. As she reminisced and cried about all her experiences in the beloved Beetle I almost felt guilty for buying it. It was hard to believe that someone could be so attached to a car.

Now, the car has belonged to me for nearly seven years. I have driven everywhere imaginable with it. Many times people have offered to buy it from me. I always say no. Everyone else who wants a VW should have a challenge in the purchase, just like me. Something so great should not be achieved so easily.

It would be too incredibly painful for me to see anyone other than myself owning the Super Beetle. I would have the same reaction as my aunt if I decided to sell the car. That would be me sitting their crying and reminiscing. Perhaps my reaction would be even stronger than hers. I do not know.

One thing's for certain: I plan to never find that out.

Tanja Ludwig

CHAPTER TWO

PARTS
& SOUL

Bugs that left a lasting impression

BUGSTRUCK

When I was a young man of the Sixties my contemporaries preferred cars that had huge engines and huge capacities for noise and fuel — Pontiac GTOs, Oldsmobile 442s, Chevy SuperSports. There was also a large number of fans of 1950s-era Chevys and Fords. Even those were modified for more horsepower to the point few Motown engineers would have recognized their original designs. Fitted with fat tires and burbling exhaust systems, these were automotive mutants; mechanical idiot savants, one-dimensional cars that were brutally strong, but lacked any refinements.

I had a secret, though, that I shared with only my closest friends. I wanted a Volkswagen Bug. They seemed to be intimate, private cars, with engaging personalities. There was a red 1966 Bug at a local dealership that I swore knew my name, that smiled and winked every time I went by. I would go over and cup the sunshine from my eyes to look at the black leatherette interior. I imagined myself sitting in the bucket seat, almost against the windshield, puttering from here to there. The sales people never bothered me, never shooed me away. I suspected they knew the longings of a 16-year-old yearning for automotive freedom. I could never swing enough money for it, or any other car at the time, for that matter. So the bus system was my ride.

In college and still Bugstruck, I only had enough money saved for a "commuter", to put it euphemistically. It was a '62 Buick Skylark that seduced me in one of those "I can afford this" moments. It was six years old, and it ran for two weeks. In retrospect, that was the best thing that ever happened to me. A football player at school had a Bug and he had just decided to sell it. It was the most beautiful car I had ever seen — a '64 Beetle with burgundy paint, carefully hand painted pinstriping and homemade wood bumpers. The brakes didn't work but I was in love. I forked over $450 and drove off, cradling the small shift knob in my hand, savoring that unique oil-flavored odor all older air-cooled Volkswagens have, listening happily to the clatter of the valves as the car accelerated, and grabbing the emergency brake at intersections. I just knew that everyone was looking at me in my Bug.

The local police insisted that the custom exhaust system be replaced with something that didn't rattle the neighbors' teeth, and I found out the hard way that a cassette radio designed for a 12-volt system doesn't work on a six-volt system, but there were few other modifications to the car. All it did was carry me around for the next three years through all sorts of weather, to all sorts of places, without complaint, always with style. I have never been attached to a car the way I was to that one.

I have owned another two dozen cars but that burgundy Bug was the standard for them all. Sure, they have air conditioning, fancy gear synchros, and more power than I could ever legally, or sanely, use but do they have that certain panache? Do they have a personality? Do they have wood bumpers or an engine that talks to you? I am saddened that my own children won't have their early automotive years spent with as good a friend as I did.

John R. Lomax Jr.

BROTHERS OF THE BUG

My father was a VW fan, as were both of my younger brothers. At one time, I believe we had at least five or six VWs of some type parked in our driveway.

My first Bug was a wine-colored '66. The year was 1976, and I was 18 years old. I purchased it for $65 from one of my father's co-workers. Not a bad deal, you say? It had no engine. The front bumper was missing, too. Not to worry. Pops soon found an engine, for which I quickly scraped up $40. The engine had been sitting in a shed next to a creek for several years. You know the story; the creek flooded and submerged the engine. But when you're 17 and the prospect of owning your own vehicle is a distinct possibility, little things like that don't seem to matter. It was running in no time. Did we rebuild it? Are you kidding? New oil, plugs, fuel filter and away I went!

That Bug evidently made an impression on my friends, for it wasn't long before they had their own. Jim had a blue one, Jeff had a red one, Mike had light blue (well, most of it was light blue) one and Tom had a, well, strange metallic green-looking thing. It kind of looked like a junebug!

And this is where the real fun began. There are so many stories, including a few I shouldn't mention here. But here goes...

One of our favorite tricks was to gather a few of us and sneak over to Tom's house late at night. We'd creep into his garage, lift the rear end of his Bug up and prop it up on bricks and boards until the rear wheels were barely above the ground. The next morning he'd jump in, start the engine and fully expect to back out of the driveway. Only his wheels would spin and spin. He'd cuss the transmission and then find out what we had done. Then he would cuss his good friends.

How about the times we heated up Jeff's driver seat? This

was a bit mean, but it was funny as heck. Jeff worked at
McDonald's. During his night shift, we'd sneak over to the
parking lot and booby-trap his Bug. We would run a single wire,
(bare on each end) from the engine coil to the drivers seat. We
tucked the wire through the space between the seat and
backrest, and made sure the exposed wire was resting on the
seat. We'd then retreat across the street, and sit and wait with
binoculars until Jeff's shift was over. He'd jump in, stick the
key in the ignition, and immediately light up like a Christmas
tree! Like I said, this one was a bit mean. But seeing his body
flail inside that Bug through binoculars from across the street
was hilarious.

I could talk about the raw biscuit fight we had one night
driving our Bugs home from Nashville to Louisville. We had
been camping a few days prior, and evidently left some of our
supplies and food in the cars. Someone discovered a few rolls of
unbaked biscuit dough in each car, and the war was on. Flinging
gooey biscuit dough at each others' Bugs at 60 mph is not
exactly the safest thing in the world, but talk about fun!
Somewhere along the way we stopped for gas and to de-biscuit
our Bugs. The dough had mostly dried out in the wind and
would not come off. Bugs with pimples. Hmm...

On another camping trip we were at a farm of one of Jim's
relatives. A few months earlier, Jim and I had been
experimenting with homemade wine. Of course, that was
required equipment for the camping trip. As soon as we arrived
at the site, which was several hundred yards through a field and
woods, we set up camp and promptly tried the wine. And tried
some more. And, well, you get the picture. In reality, the alcohol
content must not have been too strong, because I don't really
remember feeling much effect from it. But we acted like we
were staggering drunks. Before long, we were all driving our
Bugs blindly through chest-high grass in the fields, through the
woods, and over small trees. Lots of trees. At some point, we

stopped and decided to start a fire. But, here were five or six veteran campers though, without matches. We decided to drive into town for fire. It seemed like a good idea at the time.

The closest place was a small liquor store. All three of us roared up (we couldn't take just one Bug, we HAD to make a parade of it) only to find a state trooper inside. Although a bit nervous because we were under age and potentially intoxicated (at least we hoped we were), a few of us went in and coolly asked for matches. No problem. The state trooper even said goodbye to us as he waved us out the door. We were so intent on acting sober in the store, we never noticed that one of the Bugs had dragged a 20-foot-long tree into the parking lot. I can only imagine what the trooper thought as we drove away, dragging our tree back to the campsite.

I have many other stories. Stories about rebuilding a VW engine for a microbus the night before we left on a trip to Florida. Stories about spark plugs flying out of their holes while driving down an interstate only to be tapped back in and wedged in with sticks found on the side of the road. Stories about using mineral oil for an engine lubricant for thousands of miles, because it was free.

I guess the real story, now that I think of it, is the close friendship of five young men and their VW Beetles. I'm not sure any other automobile could have been a part of that.

Dave Holzknecht

BERTIE, ME OLD DARLIN'

When my Mum found out she had breast cancer, I was really distressed and went into depression for quite some time, not able to go to school or do any of the activities I enjoyed. Then, around four months later, my Dad learned he had cancer, too. Of course, this made matters 10 times worse not only for me but for all the family. We all went through hell.

Eventually, I had a reasonably large amount of money that I could use. Of course I'd already decided what I was going to spend the money on and no one could possibly stop me. I'd always adored Beetles, and learned a lot about them as I grew up. I knew a few friends who owned Beetles and I always knew that the Beetle was the car for me. On my 15th birthday I made a promise to myself that when I was old enough to drive I would never be seen in anything else!

When I put the idea to my Dad he was totally against it in every way and kept coming up with reasons not to have the car. I found this extremely frustrating. (You know how Dads can be!) So a few days later I told my Mum, and she was half-and-half about it. (You see, she had always had a soft spot for Beetles, even though she can't drive.) Well, together Mum and I persuaded Dad to go with the idea as it was the only thing that would make me happy after all that had happened. And I guess my Dad could see that the only thing that made my eyes light up was anybody mentioning the word "Beetle". And this was weird because before last year my eyes had always been ablaze with enthusiasm about almost everything. I was always described as a "sparkler of a girl" by everyone, according to my Mum!

OK. So the idea was settled! My dream was suddenly turning into a reality. But the only trouble was finding the right Beetle for me, one that didn't need too much work doing to it.

One night my friend, Graeme, brought me some copies of a Volkswagen magazine. We telephoned a few people about cars advertised in them and narrowed it down to a guy who sounded really nice, and had a cool car, too. We decided to go and have a look at it.

I can remember the vivid feelings I had, the sheer excitement of getting my first car, my dream car! I felt proud, and really grateful toward my parents for actually making it possible. We pulled around the corner of the estate where the guy with the Beetle lived. And there it was. This beautiful Bug. I knew it was definitely for me. After a tour of the car and a quick spin round we agreed on a price. Then it was mine! I couldn't believe it!

Bertie has definitely changed my life. It seems stupid, but it's true! He has cheered me up and helped bring me out of my depression. He is a truly special car and I love him to bits.

My Mum had an operation and treatment and now has a clean bill of health. My Dad also did the same, they are now both well again and enjoying life to the full. I'm having driving lessons with my Dad at the moment, on waste land of course, not on the roads. We do all the manual work on the car together. My car has given my family and I something in common which we never knew we had. It's strange just what a car is actually capable of, isn't it? All I can say is, thanks Bertie, me old darlin'!

Gemma Andrews
Felixstow, Suffolk, England

LESSONS LEARNED

I received my first driving lesson in a Bug named Annie, after the Woody Allen movie, "Annie Hall." It had an eight-track stereo! Like a Norman Rockwell painting, the family and neighbors were standing around watching me learn. My Mom guided me through the start-up procedures and instructed me to push in the clutch and put the Bug in first gear. She then told me to let out the clutch and give it some gas. I took her literally and popped out the clutch as fast it could go. The Bug violently lurched forward and went dead.

Something must have been jarred loose and the car wouldn't start again. I felt so bad for breaking the Bug less than a minute into my first driving lesson (crunching action)! Everyone was supportive but got a good laugh. Eventually the Bug was repaired and I learned to drive a standard transmission, which is becoming a dying art.

I'll never forget the sound a Bug makes. As a teenager, the distinctive sound alerted us when Mom was coming home with plenty of time to get out of any trouble we had managed to get into.

Robert Waller

LIFE IN TEEN TIMES

When I bought a 1969 VW Bug I was 18 years old. It was a four-speed. Did I know how to drive a four-speed? No, but that didn't stop me. Off I went tearing up the gears as I tried to master the fine art of driving it.

I went to the part of our community with a very steep hill. This is the hill your parents meant when they were detailing their trials and tribulations of walking to school 20 miles each way in the snow. Luckily, there was only one car at the top. Unfortunately, the driver decided to stop for the stop sign. I pulled up to that car's rear bumper as close as I could without making contact and hit the clutch and brake pedal at the same time. Everything was just fine for now. The car in front pulled away from the stop sign. Great, I thought. Then I looked in my rear view mirror and discovered there was a whole line of cars behind me. Don't panic, you can do this, I told myself.

Then I took a closer look in my mirror and much to my chagrin the car directly behind me was practically on my rear bumper. OK, panic! I did the only thing that a calm, levelheaded 18-year-old would do. I popped the clutch and hit the gas. Did I make it up the hill and through the stop sign? Of course not! My Bug stalled and started rolling back down the hill. Did I hit the brake and the clutch or just the clutch? You guessed it. By the time I did hit the brake I sheepishly glanced at my rear view mirror only to find a whole line of drivers behind me frantically trying to find reverse. With plenty of room behind me I settled down and managed to make it up the hill and through the stop sign. I could hear the cursing and cheers from the cars behind me. Nothing could stop me now.

It was so much fun owning a VW Bug in the winter, especially when it snowed. You know what I am referring to: 360s in abandoned parking lots. You also know how much fun it was trying to get the gravitation heat to warm up the car. That is, warm enough so you wouldn't have to steer with your knee on one leg, apply the clutch with the other leg, shift with one hand, while the other hand was doing — what you ask? Everyone all together now: the other hand was using an ice scraper on the *inside* of the window so you could see where you where driving. As you can imagine this put a serious crimp in your style as a stud muffin at 18.

Remember how fun it was to get into your Bug and have to loosen the clutch and brake pedals from the icebergs that had formed around them by the snow that had dropped off your boots the last time you drove it. I can remember going through this routine one winter morning in 1977 when we had wind chills at 40 degrees below zero. Did my dependable Bug start? You bet! Could I get the driver's side door to close? Now you are asking way too much. I had to drive to work holding onto the door so it wouldn't fly open. As luck would have it work shut down that day and I was sent home.

Then there was the time when I took a street corner a little too aggressively and ended up on top of a snowdrift left behind by the city's snow plows. Although the Bug's sealed bottom makes it great for floating on water it was certainly a liability on top of a snowdrift. All four wheels were suspended in space with the closest contact to payment being three feet below. Being alone, I could not dislodge it by sheer force. Luckily, I had a snow shovel in the back seat. Oh happy days!

On to more entertaining memories of my VW Bug. One night three friends and I piled into it and were on our way to some adventure when we came upon a speed bump right in the middle of a shopping center parking lot at 30 mph. Before I continue I have a question for you. Why is it that the skinny and vertically challenged teenager always gets the front passenger seat while the overweight giant teenager gets the rear passenger seat? Yeeeeowch! This blood curdling scream came from the right rear passenger seat. Where is the battery located on a VW bug? That's right. Under the right rear passenger seat. Apparently my passenger in the right rear of my Bug had come down so hard on the back seat that the springs made contact with the battery and — you got it baby. Burn baby burn! Disco inferno! Guess where the skinny, vertically challenged teenager sat from then on?

Once, on the way home from driving my girlfriend to college, my Bug started to jump all over the road. I pulled over, opened up the rear hatch protecting the engine, and peered in. The culprit was a spark plug wire, which had melted against the engine manifold. Other malfunctions: The gas tank sprang a leak. I repaired it with minimal trouble even though I had to contort myself to fit under the front hood to access the bolts to remove it. Yes, and I bragged about my accomplishments to my girlfriend, who also had a Bug. That will teach me to keep my big mouth shut. Guess whose VW had also sprung a gas leak?

The clutch cable broke a couple of times. Of course the speedometer cable broke multiple times. But overall, it was a very dependable car to drive and maintain.

I sold my Bug to my sister for $100 less than what I had paid for it four years prior. At least I thought I did. She gave me a $200 deposit and I have never, ever seen the rest. This really is not a sore subject. Honest!

Anyway, she conveyed one of her Bug memories to me. My sister and my wife (then girlfriend) once were on the way home during a torrential rainstorm. Just like how your furnace only stops working in the wintertime, the windshield wipers stopped working during this rainstorm. Luckily my sister had some gym shoes in the back seat. The girls tied the shoestrings to the two wipers, one on each side, and worked the wipers through their slightly opened windows. Synchronized swimmers would have been proud.

David Winters

HEIDI

"Damn it, Heidi. You're so stubborn. Why can't you just do what I want you to? I'm about ready beat you with a hammer. Just because you're a year older than I am does NOT give you the right to do as you please."

It was about 7:30 on a cold Chicago January morning. I was in the garage, berating my faded yellow 1971 Volkswagen Beetle named Heidi. This, if I recall, was the one morning in eight years when the little car refused to start.

When one turns 16, there is a rite of passage that we undertake called Driver's Ed. This consists of driving around town in an ugly, overweight American-made sedan with a flashing sign on the roof warning the world of your presence.

Once armed with this plastic-covered card with your picture in the corner, you are open to a new kind of freedom. Driving to school, going out with the crowd, running to the store, picking up the dry cleaning, and chauffeuring the non-driving members of the family around.

The summer of my sophomore year at Fenwick High School, I was presented with a '71 Volkswagen Beetle. My father took me into the garage late that night and solemnly told me the story of the yellow VW which sat there before me.

The car was named Heidi and officially licensed KM BUG 1. Over the next few years, Heidi taught me a lot about life that I may not have learned about otherwise.

The car came to me when I needed it most. I was at that age when I needed something to identify with; I was not popular for my sporting abilities and my grades were mediocre at best. I now became "The kid with the Beetle." I met many interesting people through Heidi. My favorite was a doctor who was a private pilot and exchanged flight lessons for the 3,000-mile tune-ups I provided for his Beetle.

Over the next several years, I put a lot of time, love, and money into my car. I rebuilt just about everything from the little tie rods in front to the tiny tail pipes in back, and loved every minute of it. It was indeed a labor of love.

I was able to piece together a brief history of the car, much of it quite by accident. An older man living in rural Southern Illinois used to walk a mile or so down the road and sit on the porch and talk about the weather with his buddies.

As time passed, he grew cranky and restless because he couldn't do the walk as often. His grandchildren realized this, so they pitched in their money and bought a shiny yellow Volkswagen so Grandpa could again have his freedom to travel. The effect on the old man was immeasurable, enough for one relative to recall how cheered he was when a granddaughter named the little car "Heidi."

Somewhere along the line, one of the grandsons bought the car from the old guy and souped it up for racing. Now Heidi, alias "Faded Lightning" was second in her class. I learned this from a guy on the pit crew.

The car changed hands a few years later when the grandson put Heidi back together and sold it to a guy named Steve. Naturally, he had grown quite attached to little Heidi during the year he owned her. So attached, in fact, that his wife placed an ultimatum before him: Either her or the Volkswagen.

One week later, the title to Heidi changed hands again, this time to me. I heard through the grapevine that Steve's wife left him a few weeks after the sale. All in all, little Heidi has had quite a past.

Heidi was always a jealous little creature. After the last owner, she never did take kindly to other women in my life. She could run for days nonstop, buying groceries and carrying me to the hardware store where I worked, but the very second she detected that a date was in progress, the yellow paint changed to an interesting shade of green.

After several bouts of exploding generators, fuel pumps that didn't, a starter that wouldn't and a horn that constantly did, I finally resigned myself to borrowing Mom's Camry for social events.

During the fourth of my six years in college I was driving home from St. Louis when I stopped near Decatur to buy some gasoline. I have grown quite used to people talking to me about my car at gas stations and such, but this one still shocks me. I was checking the oil level, when an older man using a walker went past with his grandson.

On the way back to his car, he stopped to look at Heidi. We exchanged the usual small talk about how the car looked and such, but the conversation was cut short as the younger man told the older one that it was time to leave.

As I replaced the fuel pump to the rack, I overheard the old man say, "You know, that car looks just like little Heidi."

They were gone before I realized who he was.

The time eventually came when we had to part with Heidi. That afternoon my father and I stood in the garage, going through mysterious greasy boxes filled with nuts, bolts, tools and oily things with wires attached.

It was at that time when the brick wall of reality hit us quite hard. Heidi was indeed a member of our family — my mother's first grandchild, as she put it.

We came to a very teary, emotional decision: It was time to take Heidi for one last ride. We had a great time, remembering the many VWs we test drove in the search for this one, especially our first ride in Heidi when we drove for 20 minutes before we realizing that we had absolutely no idea where we were or how to get back to return the car.

As an end to our final cruise, we stopped and picked up my Mom and sister Kerry, who was Heidi's caretaker after I bought a Honda two years earlier.

After another misty-eyed ride around town, zipping around

corners and scampering down Thatcher Avenue just like in the
old days, Heidi stopped at a dumpy little corner tavern.

We entered and ordered four of their finest German beers
and sat for a while, drinking and recalling our fondest memories
of the little car, teaching Mom how to drive a stick shift, the
time when the fuel pump gave out on my very first real date,
and driving to New York for spring break.

Heidi, I miss you. Take care of yourself, little girl, wherever
you are.

Kevin Murphy

HARRIET THE CHARIOT

I have an angel who rides with me in my car. I call him Fahrfigneugen. I've been the dubiously proud owner of a Volkswagen for only three years, but at one time or another, Fahrfigneugen has helped me out of potential speeding tickets, accidents and even an actual living, flowing creek. People tell me I am testing him. I tell them it goes along with owning a Volkswagen, in this case, a 1979 school bus-yellow convertible Beetle whom I call Harriet, short for Harriet the Chariot.

I'm not sure when my Bug/Beetle obsession began. My first memories of them are growing up in New England in the 1970s, when my best friend and I would play "Punch Buggy." Every time we spotted a Bug, we'd yell "Punch Buggy!" then the color of the car, and then do our best to bruise each other. Road trips with her were a nightmare; she was quicker and packed a harder punch.

Out west, the kids have a game called "Slug Bug," based on the idea of New England's "Punch Buggy." On my commute to the office I pass groups of kids waiting for the school bus. Depending on whether my top is up or down, I might hear someone yell "Slug Bug!" but I always see them socking each other on the arms. Despite the fact that I know some poor kid is going to end up black and blue, it gives me a goofy grin.

In high school my friends all wanted Porsches. I wanted a Bug. They didn't understand me. I didn't understand them. You could see a Porsche any day. But in New England, with its harsh winters, salted roads and salty air, Volkswagen Bugs were a rare glimpse into the past. You were lucky to see one rusting into the ground in someone's back field. And although it makes a great picture, I also hated that sight at the same time. There was just no dignity there.

I didn't get my VW as a teen. Instead I became the reluctant owner of a possessed Mazda. Only later, as an adult child when I moved out west did I finally find Harriet. She had seen better days for sure but I love her just the same.

I think my first incident involved a snapped accelerator cable. "It happens all the time. Keep three of 'em with me in mine," a friend told me. Luckily, I had Fahrfigneugen with me that day and he sputtered my car safely to the side of the road.

Then there were the gas fumes. A lot of them. "Ah, those are normal. It's a VW thing," someone else told me. But I didn't think it was normal to drive around with my top down in the winter just for fresh air, and the headaches were becoming unbearable, so I took Harriet in. It seems the seal around the gas tank was corroded. I got a lecture about toxins from my mechanic before he installed the new tank. Life was again good for Harriet and me.

But then there were more fumes. And a shaky steering wheel that had other things on its mind than keeping Harriet in between the lines. And brakes that needed some coaxing before stopping the car with an ear-piercing, screeching halt (why do all these things seem to go wrong at once?).

Back to the mechanic, who pronounced my little Harriet a deathtrap. Dumb luck had kept Harriet and me from exploding from the circa 1979 fuel lines that were leaking onto the exhaust system. Gravity and the alignment of the stars were holding the front left steering mechanism together, which at any second could have come flying off, taking with it the wheel and whatever else wanted to go. The brakes weren't there. The mechanic had no idea what was stopping the car. Fahrfigneugen had definitely been on my side.

I got a lecture about safety and car maintenance, along with some finger-shaking-in-my-face-make-me-feel-really-bad words of concern and an offer to take Harriet out to the woods and shoot her. I may have emerged unscathed, but the financial damage was bad. You know it is when the bill equals the last four digits of your phone number. Luckily, mine begins with a 1.

"When are you going to get a grown-up car?" my boyfriend would wail in exasperation. He has since refused to ride in my car even for emergency runs to the store for ice cream. He is convinced she is going to fall apart, piece by piece, leaving nothing but us sitting on the seats in the middle of the street.

His little brother, born too late in New England to ever play Punch Buggy or see a real-live Bug or Beetle, told me he thinks Volkswagens are the same as Porsches, except less expensive. Another friend insists there is a manic gnome with an eggbeater where the engine should be. This same friend and another and I went out one night to catch a show. On the way there, the brakes malfunctioned. Tail lights hurled at us at 60 mph while we imagined our impending death. Fortunately we skidded onto the shoulder just in time. To top it off, the show was canceled, and, having had enough excitement, we decided to call it a night.

Halfway home, on a lonely stretch of highway at two in the morning, Harriet wheezed, coughed and sputtered to a halt. We were out of gas. "The tank said full," I said answering in wide-eyed innocence to their glares, while making a mental note to call the mechanic about checking the gas gauge.

Luckily, Fahrfigneugen made sure that Harriet had broken down next to an emergency call box. "Do you have an adult male with you?" the somewhat nasal voice on the other end asked. I looked at my adult male friend, all five-foot six inches and 120 pounds of him. "Yes," I said. "But does it matter that I'm bigger?"

A truck was sent with gas, except the driver forgot to fill the can. I offered to call a tow truck to come out with some. He didn't think it was very funny.

After getting the gas situation straightened out and dropping my friends off, I wearily headed home. One mile from my house, I heard a high-pitched whining. I shut the radio and tried to discern where it was coming from. Then I noticed the flashing blue lights behind me. "You blew through that stop sign," a grim-faced officer, who had apparently misplaced his 3 a.m. humor, informed me. "And," he added, stepping back, "there's smoke pouring from the back of your car."

I heaved a sigh, and broke down and told him of the night's events. Of the missing brakes on the freeway. Of the concert that never was. Of the dysfunctional gas gauge. And now this, not a mile from my house.

Fahrfigneugen must have been working overtime that night, because the officer was nice enough to let me go with a warning but smart-aleck enough to recommend a mechanic.

Paula Pisani

SIGNS OF THE TIMES

In 1966 the only car I could afford was a VW. I picked out
and bought a blue one — for $1,776 — without even test
driving it, since I couldn't drive a stick shift.

My roommate's boyfriend drove the car home for me the
next day. I promptly put a sign on the back of it that said "New
Driver Stay Away!" and set out bumping and grinding to learn
how to shift for myself. After three grueling hours I didn't need
the sign anymore. I could drive it!

I loved that car and it served me well. In late 1967 I decided
to move from Kansas City, Missouri, back to Ohio to marry my
college sweetheart. When I set out on my trip, my friends made
a sign out of oilcloth that said "Cincinnati or Bust!" and
attached it to the rear bumper of my Bug. By the time I made it
to the outskirts of St. Louis, the sign caught fire since it was
hanging in front of the exhaust pipes for all those miles. It was
quickly extinguished but made for an unforgettable send-off.

Cooki Thier

THE GROOVIEST COOLER

It was May in the 1980s everywhere else but the 1960s revisited in my hometown. The local radio station announced the coming of the "Loving Feelings" concert featuring names from my youth like Gary Puckett and the Union Gap, Paul Revere and the Raiders, and Neil Diamond. Without hesitation my best friend, my crazy cousin and I jumped into the Bug and off to the civic center we went to purchase our tickets. We spent the next few weeks in anticipation and up in the attic looking for our old granny gowns, go-go boots and Nehru jackets. We weren't just going to go to the concert — we were going to become part of the concert.

A few hours before the music was to begin there were activities throughout the parking lot to promote that Sixties spirit. So the girls and I put on the Sixties rags, lined the trunk of my candy apple red, Super Beetle with plastic bags, filled the trunk with ice and loaded it with beer, wine coolers, and soda.

When we got to the parking lot, out we jumped all dressed up. POP! went the trunk to expose the biggest and grooviest ice chest around. Needless to say, we were very popular that day. Not only did we make a bunch of new friends that were very impressed with the VW-ice chest, but we won backstage passes to meet the stars of our youth!

Moral to the story: Have a VW Bug. Have an adventure. And have a nice day. Peace.

Penni Guidry

THE LITTLE BUG THAT COULD

You can't put a good man — or car — down as I learned 20 years ago when I bought a used, canary-yellow VW convertible for a bargain $1,200. Having owned tank-like American cars, I quickly discovered the pure fun of driving a devil-may-care, no fuss "Tinker Toy." I even learned to love that lawn mower-size rear engine. Sure, it wasn't Rolls Royce quiet nor did it hum like a rotary Mazda, but who could resist that eggbeater noise?

My favorite weekend pastime was donning a lifelike gorilla suit (at the time I was director of the Friends of the National Zoo), putting the top down, loading up my two young sons and our two dogs, and driving around the neighborhood. I was amazed how many people hardly noticed. Maybe gorillas driving cars around Washington wasn't any wackier than other goings-on in the nation's capital!

Of course, even a 1970 VW isn't perfect. Her one irritating quirk: after a rain, water collected somewhere in the vinyl top so when I slammed the door shut and drove off to work, water unfailingly splashed down, drenching my clothes. Heading home one day I heard an awful clattering from the rear. Positive it was just a dragging muffler, I continued driving home before checking. What I saw was amazing. It wasn't the muffler at all, but the battery that had dropped through the rusted-out support panel under the rear seat. It had been bouncing along the road all those five miles home held on by the cable! No problem. I just soldered on a new support panel, reattached the battery, and away we went. My VW was genuinely the little Bug that could — and did — always!

Sabin Robbins IV
(Portions of this story previously appeared in The Sun-Sentinel *in Fort Lauderdale, Fla.)*

MY GUARDIAN ANGELS

One of my favorite parts of owning a VW is the connection among all Bug owners. We honk and wave at each other when passing and never feel intimidated to talk to each other about our Bugs. When I owned my first Bug I always imagined a sign such as the Batman call, that would appear in the sky whenever a fellow Bug was in trouble; a Bug call.

One time my '73 Super Beetle named Mantis had a little trouble. Like in many Bugs, the gas gauge didn't work. I trusted that my boyfriend had filled the tank when he borrowed it earlier. This was a mistake. It was the last time I let him drive my Bug.

I was going up a hill on a busy street when Mantis decided that he wanted to stop. I pulled up the emergency brake but started to roll back anyway.

Quickly I turned off his ignition, threw him into first, and prayed hard that I would stay in place. I did.

I wondered what to do next. Here I was out of gas on a busy, one-lane hill. The closest gas station was some distance and I didn't have a gas container. I didn't even have any money and calling Daddy was the last resort.

Just then I heard the sound of another Bug approaching. It stopped and magically before I knew it ANOTHER Bug passed by and also stopped to help.

The two Bug owners cleared traffic on the crossing street and pushed Mantis to the nearest gas station. Without me even asking they gave me $2 for gas and left.

Sadly, I never even got their names.

As Christmas passed I wondered who they were and wished I could send them a Christmas card. I live in a small town and recognize most of the VWs here.

There aren't many that I haven't seen. Since these two men

helped me, though, I haven't sighted their Bugs anywhere.

My guess is that they were Bug-driving angels looking down on Earth for Bugs that are in trouble. Maybe they heard my Bug call.

Sarah McKinney

SISTER CLOVE

My '74 bus and I are very close. We met when I was
looking for a house to rent, there she was: her reddish orange
paint cooking in the hot sun. I had always wanted a VW bus but
never found the right one. My heart pounded with each step that
I got closer to her. I tried to balance my checkbook in my mind
so I could buy her right then and there.

I looked inside and saw all of her awesome custom work.
She had definitely been loved. Her door locks were broken so I
took it upon myself to hop in. Never had I felt so at home. The
way she smelled. The way she squeaked. The way she seemed
to hold a thousand memories. It all captured me!

It took me three months to buy her for $850. Once a week I
would go to the owner's house and sit in her, just planning all
the things we would do together.

One memory I have of her was my first night I got her
home. My boyfriend and I lit candles in her, burned incense and
listened to Tori Amos and the Grateful Dead. Later we made
love in her, as the rain poured down outside. It was incredible.
She didn't have curtains then and we had a panoramic view of
the world. The way she rocked and squeaked told me that she
had been there before and that she was happy to be back!

Within the first couple days I had named her Sister Clove. I
smoke clove cigarettes and she was definitely up for the name.

I tell everyone that Sister Clove has a soul. The first time we
took her out with six other people everyone was having a blast.
It was dark outside and I asked if anyone had some gum.

Knowing her interior lights didn't work, and as I reached for
a stick, I said "I wish I had some light in here."

Mysteriously her interior light turned on and we all laughed
hysterically at the coincidence.

My boyfriend said "No, that's nothing. If she really had a

soul she'd know that we don't need the light any more." Right on cue, she turned her lights off. I got chills in amazement. I'll never underestimate Sister Clove.

Gra´

SEALED WITH A KISS

Dear Vern:

You were eight years old when Dad brought you home. Only eight years old and you — a 1959 VW single cab pickup — looked as if you'd seen the worst the world had to offer. At the time, you weren't old enough to qualify as vintage, and you were so beat up that attempts at making you look better seemed a waste of time. Your beautification would come later, though.

Dad had always wanted a pickup, but we figured that once he actually got down to the business of buying, he'd end up with one of what everyone else had — an old Chevy, or maybe even a Ford. We were all amazed that you were what he ended up choosing. Why he picked you remains a mystery. All I know is one evening in 1967, when I was 12 years old, we set out on a short drive after dinner to bring you home. For these past 30 years, you've woven yourself into the fabric of this family's life — you have shared the fun and the pain and the difficult growing-up-times with all six of us.

My family thinks it's nutty to feel as strongly as I do about a vehicle. To them, you are a Machine. Sure, they named you and brought you closer to all of us by doing so, but they still regard you as not much more than a giant collection of nuts, bolts, and painted metal. Don't worry about that too much, OK? In their own way, they are fond of you. You have been with us so long that I think even they would hate to think of your leaving. Everyone still calls you by name and still thinks of you as the fifth child.

I wish you could talk, and tell me where you were and who had you and what you did. Who was the person that bought you when you were new, and why? I know now that whoever it was ordered you from the factory. Who mistreated you so badly and left you such a wreck? Who owned you for those eight years before we got you?

When you were first rolled off the ship in San Francisco, Eisenhower was president, Alaska and Hawaii became states, and the minimum wage was $1 an hour. A new house had an average price tag of $12,400, a gallon of gas cost 25 cents, and "Ben Hur" won Best Picture of the year. Ford officially declared its Edsel a flop. I was five years old, and my baby brother (who is a chef now, lives in Chicago and has three children) was a toddler at two years old. My Mom and Dad had only been married for 15 years, and would go on to spend a happy total of 47 years together. Volkswagen was certainly not an unknown in the United States at that time, but it was not the presence it would later grow to be.

I remember taking one look at that broad, blue face of yours and knowing I was in love. I would never let someone else have the fun that you were and still are. I remember many happy trips spent with you ticking off the miles. Do you remember that rainy Saturday when you, Dad, Jill and I traveled up to the ranch, 200 miles away? It rained so hard your poor leaky windshields couldn't take it any more and the water ran down the dash until Jill and I stuffed Kleenex in the disintegrating rubber to stop it. Do you remember that horrible, hot July at the same ranch, hauling all of us (except Mom, who refused to ride in your bed) to the ballpark to watch the fireworks? I thought we had the best seats around, sitting on lawn chairs in your bed, high above those sitting on blankets on the ground. I also recall a certain wild goose chase that Dad made, piloting you up some narrow, unknown dirt road in the rain. Why? Just because you'd never been up there before. The rain got heavier, the road got muddier, and before we knew it, your rump had slipped off one side and your back tires were mired in a ditch. Of course, you had no intention of staying there in that ditch, so with Dad carefully driving and the rest of us easing your hiney out, you crawled out of that muddy ditch on your own and we headed back to safety. You never let us down.

Oh! And how about that time in San Francisco when your BRAKES went out? That was exciting! Your poor mechanical parts could never seem to keep up with your brave heart. You always had the gumption, it was just sometimes hard for your old parts and pieces to keep pace. So many times you limped home with us inside, and I don't recall ever worrying too much that you might not make it. You always did.

That terrible night in 1973 taught me that you were a real friend. If I doubted it before, I didn't after that. I can remember my surprise at seeing that Toronado come out of nowhere and smash into your side, narrowing missing me in the driver's seat. It was late, around 1 a.m., and I must have been sleepy to pull out in front of that speeding behemoth. The impact really hurt you, I could tell that immediately. Your side was ripped open, your engine case and battery smashed, your gas tank ruptured and axle broken. But we both went on, a bit battered and but a lot wiser, too. That wreck made me a better driver, and made me more determined than ever not to lose you.

Cars that arrived in our driveway since you came to live with us came and went, but you remained. The unthinkable happened in 1974 and still you persevered: I brought home a usurper to your affections, my '69 VW Bug. Of course, by this time you were getting on in years and needing a lot more than I could comfortably afford. Once I got a real job I needed reliable transportation (and, I thought, a real stereo) and the most logical conclusion was to buy a "real" car. Dad kept you after this, then sold you to someone I knew: my boyfriend. Rob thought you were cool and needed something to haul his dirt bike around in. I would still get to see you. And, since you were now Rob's truck, I might even get to drive you now and then.

Rob took good care of you and was kind to you. You helped him move into his first and second apartments. You helped his brother move. Then, when Rob and I got married, you helped move ME into my new home. Once again, you and I were linked. We had a mostly uneventful life after this, unless you want to count the time that I tried to sell you. I knew you were against it right from the start. I had that guy wanting to buy you but he must have sensed my hesitation because he didn't give me a deposit right away. He asked me to call him back after we'd made the deal because he wanted to be sure I was OK with selling you. After a week or so of nightmares about you leaving I called him back. I just couldn't do it. The dents and rust and decay didn't matter. I'm glad the guy understood.

We won't even talk about your restoration. By the time I borrowed the money to make this happen, you were such a part of me that I couldn't have stopped this if I'd tried. I don't need to remind you how it felt to see you sitting there, in the shop, with all your new paint and chrome and that big smile! Did you ever look like a happy truck! I hope you also felt how much you meant to me, surely you realize that was why I did what I did. Dad died in 1991, but he got to see the fun I had restoring you, and he also got to see his old beat-up work truck turned into a glorious work of art. That summer evening he first saw you, he took one look and then looked at me, his pride obvious. Dad was about the only one besides Rob that really knew what you mean to me.

I cried a bit when I wrote this, happy tears some, but mostly just from the nostalgia of remembering you. Don't worry, I'm not sad. Vern, the last 30 years have really been a kick. I sure am looking forward to the next 30. Stick around, I guarantee you'll enjoy our ride. And please don't think I'm a sap. No, I'm not a sap, I'm just in love — in love with an old blue truck.

Love,
Your Mom

Lois E. Grace
(Portions of this story previously appeared in The Autoist*)*

GET AWAY- GIVE AWAY

It's funny the things you remember about a particular car you once owned; how it reminds you of times, and people, and feelings.

When I got out of the Navy, near the end of the Vietnam War, I was driving a well-worn 1952 Beetle convertible. The faded yellow paint job was more compatible with the tired engine than it was with the decent body and interior.

With the vast number of returning veterans looking for employment, jobs were scarce. After searching for several months, I was finally hired as a bill collector for a finance company. My collection territory was South-Central Los Angeles, in the area known as Watts.

My little Beetle would carry me the 30 miles from my home in Orange County to the office in L.A. I got good mileage, and the nearly two-hour commute was fairly comfortable with the top down.

You can imagine how out of place a young guy wearing a suit, driving an old VW would appear in that neighborhood just a few years after the riots of 1965.

One fall afternoon, I made a call on a client who lived in a typical stucco bungalow on a street deep in the neighborhood. As I recall, the guy didn't owe much; he just hadn't made a payment in six months. I pulled up to the curb and parked my Beetle with the top down, it did no good to lock it. I kept it in view as I walked up to the porch. I knocked on the door and stood back, waiting for the owner to answer.

Evidently he'd seen me coming (or I looked like a bill collector) because he tore open the door and started yelling at me. If he hadn't had trouble with the lock on the screen door, I might not have gotten the head start I needed. I quickly backed down the sidewalk, turning as I got to the curb, jumped over the door of the Bug and started up the tired little engine.

By this time, my pursuer was moving as quickly as he could, still yelling obscenities, and waving his cane at me. He'd almost reached the car as I pulled away at lightning (?) speed. As I made my getaway, I could see him in the rearview mirror — waving his cane. I was almost afraid he'd catch me.

Shortly afterward, I traded my little car for a Pontiac GTO. Then, in 1976, I bought a like-new '69 Beetle from the original owners. They'd religiously had the car serviced and, in fact, had kept every service slip in the glove box. This perfect little car was great for my daily commute into work, it was easy to maintain, and I owned it free and clear.

When I discovered I was being transferred from Southern California to Iowa, I still planned to take the car with me; that is until the pastor of our church told us of a problem he was having. Here was a man who was married and had three children (one disabled and one an infant). He also had an incurable stomach ailment. Then, to make matters worse, his worn-out car had finally died. He was left with no transportation and no means of acquiring any.

It's interesting how God speaks to a person. When I heard the pastor's story, I knew I needed to give him the VW. I didn't want to, but I knew I needed to. I told him about my decision and we made plans to carry out the transaction.

Over the years I've often wished that I still had that perfect, showroom-floor car, but then I'm reminded of how "perfect" it was for this needy man and his family. I know I did the right thing.

Bruce L. Wilson

CHAPTER THREE

HOW I GOT LOST ON THE ROAD LESS TRAVELED THEN FOUND INSTANT KARMA ON I-96

Bug tales of the road

A GENTLEMAN'S WANDERLUST

I had lived in an apartment for several years and I always had a need to get out of that small area. I would get in the car — a 1969 Bug — and go drive in the countryside for two or three hours at a time. I did this quite regularly.

Then I met someone who went to Nova Scotia to teach at one of the universities in Halifax in the summer. She got me interested in maybe going there. So for about five weeks each summer in '74 and '75 that's what I did. I took my time getting there and getting back. I even went up by Montreal and Quebec City and crossed over a ferry into New Brunswick and then drove into Nova Scotia and down to the south shore. I went all around the island. I just found it a wonderful place and when I figured out how to rig the car up so I could stay in it, camping was so convenient.

I took the passenger seat out, and then I got two four-by-fours, some 3/4-inch plyboard and some hook latches. Then I got some two-inch foam rubber and I had a "bed" I could put my sleeping bag on at night yet take apart during the day and pile onto the back seat. It worked out so well. I had a very comfortable place to sleep.

When I put the sleeping arrangement away for the day I put a basket for food and utensils where the passenger seat had been. And I had an ice chest. I also traveled with a little propane tripod stove and the gas tank actually served as one of the legs to it, so it didn't take much space.

So I could keep the sunroof open and not have to worry about insects I got a nice long piece of nylon mesh that went all across the top of the car and came into the windows on either side. Then I sewed heavy lead sinkers — like you use for fishing — in the ends of it so it would hold it down and stretch it tight. I could roll up the windows so that it would be very stable. I could open the sunroof and look up at the stars through the mesh. When I'd get ready to go to bed at night I'd spray a little bug spray in there for extra protection.

Looking up at the stars though the sunroof was one of the nice things about camping like this because a lot of the camping spots were not very busy. You could be very, very alone and it would be so quiet, especially if you were near the ocean and you could hear the surf and things like that. It was just idyllic.

One time I was down on the south shore and I got caught in rain and fog that lasted for three days. I'd made contact with some fishermen who were going to let me go out with them on their boat for the day but the weather prohibited it. So I waited. Canada has good classical music on their FM stations and since it was cool outside, I stayed in the car and listened to music and read and did things like that. I could fix a meal right there without having to get out in bad weather. For about three days I holed in like that. It wasn't that bad. I rather enjoyed it because it's something you don't usually do. But I gave up after three days.

During my trips I met some interesting people and the Bug itself attracted a good bit of attention, when people saw what was happening. One time, coming back, I was spending the night in Acadia National Park in Maine and it was extremely crowded. It didn't really look like a camping situation; it was too crowded for that. Everybody just had enough room for their car and their tent and of course, I didn't take up any room but for the car primarily. There were places where you could walk around so when people saw me rigging it up for the night, they came over and the word spread. Sometimes even after I had gone to bed they'd come up and look. My arrangement was a novelty and I loved it.

Marcus Jordan

INTERCONTINENTAL CAMPING

My husband, Richard, and I had "dropped out of society" and begun traveling around Europe with our toddler, Jason. We bought a VW camper while we were in Holland.

We got it at a place at the airport because there was a tax break; you didn't have to pay taxes on it until you came back to the United States. It was an orange, '73 model with a pop-up top — our son loved the color. It had an icebox instead of a refrigerator and no stove. There was, however, a little sink with a hand pump. We were going to be able to move around and live in the van at the same time. This couldn't have been any more perfect for Jason because he was only two feet away from his parents the whole time. (A funny thing happened much later after we came back to the U.S. and got ready to move into a house. We told our son — who'd only known an apartment and the VW as his homes before — "OK, you can pick your room." And he went to the closet. He really did. Apparently he felt most comfortable in a small, compact area.)

Anyway, I was always very picky about where we camped. One time we drove into a campground in France. It had a lot of concrete and we drove around until we found a tree. The tree happened to have been near some grass, and then a parking area where there were some cars facing us.

We pulled up by an identical orange VW camper and, literally, we were right next to each other. Jason went outside by the tree and a little French boy about his age was there and they both started talking and jabbering like 3-year-olds. The boy's parents were also looking out the window of their camper and the next thing we knew, both boys had pulled their pants down. I don't even know if they got to urinate, if they even made it that far. But they just stood there and stared at each other's penises. It was hysterical. And the next thing we knew they both got very upset and just ran to their respective campers.

We sat in the camper and explained to Jason about why the other little boy looked that way, and about circumcision and so on. We could only assume the exact same conversation had to be going on over there, like a mirror image only in French. And then after a little bit they both went outside and started playing again. You didn't have to speak the same language to understand. The children were OK and would just play together anyway.

Another memorable time was when we had been to Denmark and back through Germany and back to Holland. It was late at night and somebody told us there was a campground "down that way" so that's where we headed. We had been in the camper for about four months at that point, and were getting pretty experienced. We couldn't find anybody at the camping area we'd been directed to but we figured it was no big deal so we pulled off the road and got ready for bed. I don't think we even put the top up. But we had the curtain around the front window. Our son was on his cot; that was like a king-sized bed for him.

The next morning Richard woke up to the sound of muffled voices. He looked out the window on one side and there was a whole soccer team lined up, ready to play. He thought something seemed funny about that so he looked out the other side and there was another team. We were dead center in the soccer field without knowing it and they were ready to start playing! But nobody had woken us. The Dutch players were very polite; they were just waiting. We quickly got everything ready and Dick said "I'll pull the curtain, start the motor and we're out of here." As we left everybody started clapping and cheering.

That VW truly was our home. Whenever we would meet someone else with one we'd talk about how they'd customized it and made it their own. Some people had lamps and antiques in theirs. We'd share meals, play cards and talk. An Irish friend taught us songs. In Portugal we celebrated a birthday and even had a tiny cake with a candle. Sometimes other Americans we'd meet

would celebrate holidays with us, like Thanksgiving or Christmas dinner. So many things happened around that little table in our camper.

While we were in Germany we even toured the plant where the camper was made. We also went to Poland, Morocco, the Mediterranean regions, Spain, Czechoslovakia, and so on. One time we were free camping and the "la guardia" started coming around and asking questions. When they got to us Jason spoke to them and they loved it. They put their guns behind their backs and went on to rousting the other campers. I don't think we knew for sure what they wanted.

We kept a scrapbook of pictures and things from our travels. Later, the VW sat in the garage and our son learned to drive on it. Our daughter — who was born after we returned to the States and has heard our wonderful memories for years — is sentimental about everything. She was really upset when we finally got rid of the camper. She hoped we'd keep a seat or something....

Bella Nomberg Golden and Richard Golden

TORTOISE AND THE HARE

I used to have to travel from Denver to Albuquerque, New Mexico about twice a week. At the time I had a classic muscle car: a '69 Javelin AMX.

Once I was cruising down the road at about 95 mph when up ahead in the distance there was a shiny little red Bug puttering along at only about 55. I quickly closed the distance and saw it was being driven by an older woman. She disappeared from my rear view mirror quite quickly and I didn't think much of it.

Soon I needed fuel. While filling up my monster, I watched that same Bug pass on by the station. Within minutes I was blasting down the road once again. Some time went by and I caught up with the now familiar Bug, passing it for the second time. Before I knew it, the fuel gauge was getting close to the "E" mark again. I pulled into a gas station. Right on cue, that little old lady passed by again. I could hardly stand the irony as I passed her again.

The third time I filled up was just outside Albuquerque, when over the rise and into the parking lot turned that little red Bug. The woman went right past the fuel pump and parked at the curb. She got out, mopped her forehead with a handkerchief, walked up to the soft drink machine and got a drink. She gave me a little smile as she got into her Bug again and continued on.

James B. Johnson

WHAT THE HELL ARE TOPAS?

On vacation in Cancun Mexico in 1990, my wife and I rediscovered something we already knew. We weren't sit-on-the-beach-and-soak-up-some-rays kind of people.

Being a life-long VW guy who was Bugless for over three years, I was delighted to see just how popular the new Mexican Beetles were with the locals. They were everywhere. My wife and I agreed that this would be a great opportunity to introduce her to the pleasures of Bugging. We'd rent one and go explore the Mayan ruins in the surrounding area.

Being "gringos" with a high school level of Spanish fluency we felt it would be prudent to find out just how safe this idea of ours really was. We quickly learned that the hotel clerks were well rehearsed in their answer.

They all felt it was *muy dangerous* to rent a car and travel alone due to the dreaded *banditos*. Fortunately, they each knew a guy who ran a tour company that could get us to our desired destinations unscathed by the fearsome banditos who prey on Americano VW fans in search of Mayan ruins. It would only cost us.... you get the picture.

We got wise to the scam after three identical answers and decided to ask the regional authorities. We soon found a police officer that spoke enough English to tell us the real scoop.

The highways to Tulum and Chichen Itze were safe as long as we used some common sense. He dispensed with some time-tested advice such as: if you see someone wearing a mask and carrying a gun who is appears to be broken down by the side of the road DON'T STOP. With this advice we couldn't be stopped. We set out to rent a new 1990 Bug.

We went in the first car rental agency we came to that had a well-stocked corral of shiny new '90 Bugs. Upon going inside we stated our intentions. Roger (locally pronounced Rowyer), our rental agent, immediately proclaimed, "You don't want one of them, you want something with air conditioning."

Insisting that we really did want a Bug, Rowyer admitted he too was a Bug fan but the company makes him try to upgrade customers. We chose a white one, filled out the mandatory paperwork and were ready for our adventure.

Upon sharing our plans Rowyer gave us one of those puzzled "You Americanos really find that entertaining?"kind of looks. He asked if we had ever been "snorneling.." Snorneling?, we asked. What's snorneling? It seemed Rowyer knew a guy who ran a snorkeling company and he could get us lessons. It would only cost us...yeah, we know. It seemed like everybody knew a guy and it will only cost you....

Our Mexican VW road trip was about to begin. Our first day was at Tulum, a Mayan ruin on the coast some 90 miles south of Cancun. The trip was a delight. Now my wife finally understood the appeal of Bugs. She fell in love with the car we'd rented. The next day it was time to take a real trip. We headed for Chichen Itze.

Chichen Itze is one of the most famous Mayan ruins in Mexico. It would be a journey of roughly 200 miles into the center of the Yucatan Peninsula. We set out on what the police officer referred to as "the highway". It was actually a narrow, two-lane road cut between the tropical overgrowth. The road signs were literally painted on boulders along side of the road.

Fairly certain that spending the night in a Mexican prison wasn't the kind of adventure we wanted, we drove at what we felt to be a quasi-legal speed. It became apparent that we were the only ones concerned with the speed when we were passed by a beat up semi pulling three trailers on a blind curve of this two-lane "highway".

Recovering from the blast of wind and deafening noise "Mad Max" created when he passed, we figured speeding up was the thing to do.

Thinking the semi was the biggest scare we could get that day, we began to get comfortably bored on the long trip. The VW's speedometer read in kilometers. Looking down I commented how it made it look to the American eye like we were going much faster.

Being the pranksters that we were, we thought it would be funny to take a picture of the dashboard with the speedometer needle buried well into the triple digits. I mean it obviously was a Beetle dash and nobody had to know the speedometer was reading kilometers. They'd see the picture and think we hit a new land speed record in a Bug. This was a great idea, our mothers would be horrified when they saw this!

We sped up until the Bug could go no faster. My wife prepared to take the incriminating photo. It was at this time we saw a rare sight, an actual road sign. It was small but it was a road sign and not a painted rock. It said "TOPAS".

That was a word I never encountered in high school Spanish. We quickly got back to our intended photo. Then suddenly another sign that read "TOPAS".

Before I could get out the words "What the hell are TOPAS?" we were taught an unforgettable Spanish lesson. Apparently TOPAS are very large rounded yellow speed bumps that crest about six inches above the roadway. Their intended use is to force trucks on this "highway" to slow down to a crawl as they enter the outskirts of a village.

We found a new use. At the equivalent of about 78 mph, TOPAS form a near-perfect launching device for a rented VW Beetle. Busily trying to figure out the sign, we hit the TOPAS with incredible force.

The crash of violently recoiling suspension, blood curdling screams and the roar of the over-revved VW motor filled the air as the back wheels followed the front ones skyward. We got some serious air.

After what seemed like an eternity, we hit the ground with a bone-jarring thud. The jolt nearly tore the steering wheel out of my hands.

About a quarter of a mile after landing, I brought the Beetle/light aircraft to a stop. With no apparent damage to the VW and minimal bruising to our bottoms, we continued on to our destination. Not much older but forever wiser. For we had learned a new word. In Spanish, TOPAS may mean speed bumps, but for us it will always mean flying Bug.

Paul Klebahn

22 DAYS OF AMERICA

It's tough to look back and not miss both the era and the van. It seems as if they were symbolically connected, as if one could not have existed without the other. Then, throw in the fact that I was coming of age — you know, sexual awareness meets wanderlust. Dangerous combination.

It was a 1969 maroon VW camper van. I still see one from time to time. Beige plaid curtains. Tan plastic/vinyl seats. Pop-up top. The manual said it slept a bunch of people in a weird configuration of rigs and such. I never needed to sleep more than two.

I got it in '74. Had it 'til '76. I bought it used from Charlie, my mother's second husband. Seems it broke down in Little Rock and he left it to be repaired while he flew home to Cincinnati. Now he needed someone to fly to Arkansas and drive it back.

My best friend, Jeff, went with me and we had our first adventure in the van I had just learned how to drive a stick shift and was still a little rough in first gear. More than a little rough, so Jeff and I devised a plan. He would get us up to speed on the interstate then move over and drive from the passenger's side while I slid into the driver's seat and took control. When I tell people this story they have one of two reactions. Many comment on how dangerous it was. Then there are those who owned VW vans. They're the ones who say "Yeah, I used to do that, too."

When I arrived home, Charlie offered to sell the van to me. I mastered first gear. I was hooked. I was unstoppable.

I wasn't the guy with the "Don't laugh, It could be your daughter I have in here" bumper sticker. I didn't even have one that said "Don't bother knockin' when this van is rockin". Sure, I still think of some of the girlfriends who'd joined me in the van. But the real memories have more to do with the wanderlust. The freedom. No longer being under my parents' roof. No longer asking permission to plan my life.

Jeff and I are now in our early 40's, each with two sons, one wife, and our own businesses. But we were inseparable in those days and we still carry a lot of the summer of '74 with us.

It was the lean years for diehard Cincinnati Reds fans. There had not yet been a "Big Red Machine" that won two World Series in a row. We were still hoping for days like that to come and we weren't going to take a chance on missing them. We were rabid Reds fans with a van and tickets to games in Houston, Los Angeles, San Diego and San Francisco. The first game would be in the Astrodome on Wednesday night. We left on Sunday.

We removed the refrigerator which had stopped working years before and filled a cooler with food. Space was important as we left on our 22-day adventure. We packed some clothes. A map. And $600. Six hundred dollars for two college students to drive, eat, sleep and experience 22 days of America. No direction. No plans. No problems.

As we pulled away from Jeff's house I said the words that would define the trip. "Where do you want to go?" He unfolded the map of the country and surveyed possibilities in all directions. "I've never been to New Orleans," he said. So we headed south.

The van was our home. It was diner and hotel. We ate, slept talked and sang. It carried us past sites we had only seen in books.

It carried us to the French Quarter of New Orleans. In Galveston we slept on the banks of the Gulf of Mexico. It was our first look at the Rocky Mountains and the desert southwest. It took us to Las Vegas, the Grand Canyon, Hoover Dam, and Mexico. We saw Fisherman's Wharf, Universal Studios and, of course, all those Reds games.

Thursday morning sunrise over the Gulf of Mexico. We had seen the Reds beat the Astros in Houston the night before — in spite of almost being no hit by Don Wilson. We watched the sun come up, played on the beach and then it was "The Question" time again. "Where do you want to go?"

Jeff, the do-or-die baseball guy, wanted to cross northern Texas so we could check out the Texas Rangers' stadium and maybe see another ball game. I wanted to touch history.

"Let's cross south and stop in San Antonio. We can see the Alamo," I suggested. I won.

I had never seen it before so the only imagery I had came from movies. That's why I assumed we'd probably have to find our way out in the desert. There, we'd no doubt see the Alamo in the distance. The van carried us closer as we talked of Davy Crockett and John Wayne.

It was just after five in the afternoon when we pulled into San Antonio. The September sun was setting low in the sky. What a beautiful sunset it would be over the sand-roughed ruins of history. Jeff leaned out the passenger side window to ask a business man for directions to the Alamo. "Two blocks down, take a right."

We drove the two blocks and turned. There it was. In the middle of town. Squeezed between a Mom-and-Pop restaurant and a t-shirt stand. There was no desert. There was no history. Crowded urban America had swallowed up our vision of history. And the worst part? It was closed. The Alamo closed at 5 p.m. We drove all the way across Texas to see the Alamo and it was closed. We could be at a ball game but nooooooo. We had to see the Alamo. Jeff was beside himself with the irony and awareness of the opportunity to razz me about this for years.

It is a picture that time has not faded. We drove out of San Antonio with Jeff leaning through the van window shouting his parting words: "Remember the Alamo."

I wish the story ended there. It didn't. A little before

midnight — after seven hours of "Remember the Alamo" —
Jeff decided to sleep and I took the last driving shift to get us to
the New Mexico border.

Then I saw a sign for the grave of Judge Roy Bean. History!
I was finally going to see history. I was sure Pecos, Texas was
still a small little desert town — probably few buildings maybe
a monument and a museum dedicated to Lily Langtree just like
I saw in the Paul Newman movie.

About 2 a.m. Jeff rolled over as I pulled off the main drag.
"Where are we?"
"Almost there."

He went back to sleep. Good thing. When I finally found the
judge's grave site there was nothing there but a tombstone.
Disappointed, I turned the van west and hurried out of town.

In Las Vegas, we slept at Circus Circus Hotel. Actually we
slept in the van in Circus Circus Hotel parking lot. We lost $50
of our $600 at the gaming tables within 30 minutes of getting
into town. Another lesson learned. Short stay in Vegas.

One day, miles from nowhere in the middle of Wyoming, we
were running low on gas. There in the distance — a gas station.
Saved! As we got closer I uttered another phrase that I'll long
remember. "76 cents a gallon? I'd rather run out of gas than pay
76 cents a gallon." I miss those days, too.

The van also carried souvenirs of our trip. Seashells from
the banks of Lake Pontchartrain in New Orleans. Hanging moss
from the big Louisiana trees. Pinatas from Tijuana. Once we
sneaked into Dodger Stadium and grabbed a handful of dirt
from the outfield warning track. As we drove away we saw the
real prize: A parking divider with Dodger Stadium painted on it.
What is the statute of limitations on stealing a sawhorse-type
parking divider? If it's passed then here's my confession. Jeff
stole it. I was merely the accomplice. I drove past while Jeff
leaned out the side sliding door and grabbed it as we passed.

Last stop: San Francisco. After the cold September night

game at Candlestick — money almost gone, time running out — we decided it was time to head for home. We drove from San Francisco to Cincinnati in less than 48 hours. For those without a calculator that's an average of more than 55 miles an hour.

We used the Little Rock trip switch method for changing drivers. We stopped only for gas, bathroom purposes and hamburgers before revving the van back up to 65. By that time, it was beginning to chug and wheeze.

We made it back to Cincinnati, dropped Jeff at his house and I headed home. The van died before I completed the five-mile trip to my house. It served us well but now it needed a tow and a tune-up.

I drove the van for two years after the trip. In 1976 I got a serious job and needed a more serious ride, a '76 Buick Century. I never bonded with that car.

Jeff and I still laugh about the VW days. It's funny but we both have mini-vans now. But they're the kind for hauling soccer kids and garden mulch and taking the kids and dogs to Grandma's house. And there are times when Jeff and I look at our lives and our mini vans and our sons and wonder "What if Zach and Tyler and Alex and Sam wanted to take the mini van for 22 days of discovering America. Wouldn't that be great?"

And I think about the Alamo and the Gulf of Mexico and Judge Roy Bean and smile. Then I think about several memorable women friends I shared the van with. No way will my kids ever leave the house until they're married.

On second thought, Jeff and I will go with them for another round of discovery. Where do you want to go?"

Jim Friedman

CHRISTMAS IN BETHLEHEM

I purchased my first Bug in late September of 1969. I was a first-year teacher making $6,000 annually. I needed a car that was economical, low maintenance and dependable. A red VW Beetle perfectly fit all my needs. Even though I splurged and ordered only two options — a radio and a cigarette lighter — my payment was only $63 per month. My annual percentage rate was only 2.5%!

The car immediately became my best friend. Every weekend was a road trip to see friends within a 300-mile radius. My "VeeDubber" became a symbol of my independence, but also my revolt against conventionalism. I didn't need flash or panache. The Bug got me where I wanted to go efficiently, economically, and with little fanfare. I loved that car with the same passion that I loved my first job, my first apartment and being a 22-year-old idealist who was going to change the world.

My parents had moved to Albany, New York, some 670 miles from where I was living. I didn't get to visit them until Christmas vacation. I planned to drive straight through on Christmas Eve. Everything went well until I reached Syracuse, where it started to snow very heavily.

I was about 100 miles from Albany. The New York State Thruway (I-90) was under about six inches of snow in most places and 10 inches in others. The only other traffic on the road was large trucks. I followed their tracks and lights to stay on the road. The Bug never faltered although I could barely go 40 mph because of poor visibility.

It was well past my estimated time of arrival and approaching midnight when I finally saw the Albany exit. I had already been on the road for 16 hours. I was dead tired; my back and butt were killing me and my hands were numb from the steering wheel vibration.

Somehow I took a wrong turn off the exit and headed away from Albany. After a few minutes I began to realize that something was wrong. It was still snowing very hard and I was out in the middle of nowhere. Suddenly I saw a sign: "Welcome to Bethlehem".

The irony of arriving in Bethlehem at midnight on Christmas Eve did not escape me. I stopped at the first lighted building that I came to; got directions; and arrived at my parents' house shortly thereafter. The next morning I awoke to find my beloved Bug completely buried by the snowstorm. What a Christmas!

As I grew older, more prosperous, married and comfort-seeking, I outgrew my succession of Beetles (I've owned three). Every now and then I see one on the road and remember fondly what great cars they were and how I loved them. The unpretentious Beetle: the perfect car for someone like me.

Bill Schmidbauer

STRANGER IN A STRANGE LAND

In 1961, I was moved to Morocco with my wife and 10-month-old baby for my job on a military base. About a month later, once we got into base housing, we decided we needed a car. I'd always heard good things about VWs and there was a Volkswagen agent on base. We decided to get one. It was a turquoise '62 with no radio. It was really a nice car. It only cost $1,350.

I had not been off the base much at that time and had never driven in a foreign country, nor had I ever driven a VW, but I had to go about 25 miles to Casablanca to pick up the car. After I had the paperwork arranged, a sergeant who could speak some Arabic took me to the dealership. Fortunately the sergeant had a VW and a Porsche and was able to give me a quick training course on how to drive the car because the dealer offered none. He was able to get me going although I was a bit nervous knowing I'd have to drive through the Casbah to get to the main highway.

For those who've never seen "Casablanca" the Casbah is a narrow-streeted marketplace crowded with people and camels. You could get lost in there for days. I thought back to the base's orientation and how we were warned about the harsh ramifications of hitting pedestrians or livestock in that country. I don't think I got it out of first gear for a number of miles. So there I was surrounded by bikes, donkeys, people and camels going through this mass while driving my shiny new VW for the first time. I was scared but I made it.

My wife quickly learned how to drive the car and fell in love with it. Our kids were brought up with it and loved it, too.

In 1963, we were moved to Germany and we had the little turquoise Bug shipped back more less to where it came from. We bought a small camping trailer and we mounted a rack to the top of it to carry a playpen and other paraphernalia. We planned a trip from our home in Bremerhaven, to Rome, Italy. We slowly but steadily chugged up through the alps in Switzerland. The poor VW stayed in second gear for most of climb.

Once on top of the mountains we were told that you could see four countries. Not this day. By the time we reached the peak, the fog was so thick you couldn't see out the windshield. There were no guardrails on the right side either, only a shear drop-off. I had to roll down the window and stick my head out to look for the white line on the road in order to safely proceed.

Finally, on our descent through Gotthard Pass, the fog broke. You could see over the drop-off on the right. It was a long way down. We slowly followed the narrow road around sharp curves that were cut into the mountain's side.

We started around one curve and were surprised by a wide truck coming up the other side. It was apparent that we both weren't going to fit. Both the truck and I stopped. The driver got out and motioned me to go around him. I felt there wasn't enough room and there was no way I was getting my family any closer to the unguarded cliff inches from the side of the road. I surely wasn't about to try to back the trailer up next to a cliff, either. I refused to go.

I could clearly see that the truck had a back-off spot directly behind him. The traffic was now lined up behind the truck just as it was behind me. I couldn't understand the truck driver and he couldn't understand me but judging by his red face and shaking fist, I assumed he was none too pleased and he wasn't backing down, either.

A half hour of multilingual cursing later, the police came. Fortunately for me, the police made the truck back down and we were on our way again.

We always got the most out of that little car. One time some friends of ours with a large family were leaving the country and had no transportation to Frankfurt, Germany, their departure city. There were seven of them and six of us. Fortunately for the sake of our friendship, most of the kids were small and we didn't have to go too far. Everyone survived.

After driving the car for many years in Morocco and Germany, I began to experience a problem with the steering. I sought out a reputable mechanic and was directed to his shop about 20 miles from our home. The owner was everything I came to expect from a German mechanic. He was clean and meticulous. After giving him ample time to diagnose the problem, he summoned me into the work area with a scowl on his face. I could tell he was upset. He showed me how a piece in the steering mechanism had worn because it had never been greased since the car was new. Like a veterinarian accusing a farmer of abusing his work horse, he lectured me. He told me he felt it was a disgrace that I hadn't cared for the car better. I actually felt guilty.

This wonderful little turquoise Bug was our family's only means of transportation until 1968 when we bought a new VW bus to share the load of our growing family. In '69, we were to move back to the United States and we had to make a tough decision. We could only have one vehicle shipped so we had to sell the Bug. We really shed some tears over that. It had truly become part of the family. We really missed it.

Dick Imhoff

JOCKEYING FOR ATTENTION

In the spring of 1972 my friend Dan and I were living in East Palo Alto, California. Dan was moving back to Ohio and I was returning for my sister's wedding. Because the wedding was just a few days off, we decided to drive straight through wondering if we might set a record for the quickest Bug trip across the country.

While standing around in my underwear waiting for our laundry to dry we determined it not likely anyone had driven across the "fruited plains" in their underwear. Someone said "I dare you" and that was enough. We loaded up "Jethro", my Labrador/Husky, and the three of us lit out for the Buckeye State.

We didn't make many stops along the way other than for gas but everyone we did meet along the way gave us an approving smile and a thumbs up, even when we weren't able to tell them just what we were up to. There really wasn't much to tell. We were just two guys going cross-country in our underwear on a dare. With a dog.

Thirty-seven hours later, much to everyone's surprise, we arrived back home. In time for my sister's wedding. In my B.V.D.s. In a Volkswagen.

Sadly, Jethro is no longer "with us" to substantiate our tale.

Joe Singler

CHAPTER FOUR

A WING
AND A SPARE

Breakdowns, fixes, and making it home

CANNONBALL!

It was a warm Monday in early July, 1986 — my birthday as a matter of fact. The road was my home. I was driving a '74 Super Beetle, which I had been warned did not belong outside of city limits. But there I was, already at the border of North/South Carolina and not a problem in sight. After a quick pit stop at the local rest area I prepared to make my grand entrance at Myrtle Beach.

Bump. Bump. Clatter. Bump. What's this? A flat, no doubt, I assured myself while pulling over into the nearest stop. But alas, the left front tire seemed fine, practically bursting with air. I must have hit something in the road I told myself. I was too close to my destination for any small inconveniences to derail my vacation now.

I pulled back onto the main road, smelling the salt air. I checked my speed. There was no need to get a ticket now in my haste to mingle with Southern belles and cold beer. It seemed like I was going quite fast but my speedometer registered zero. Hey, wait a minute! Wasn't my speedometer cable attached to my left front wheel? The one I had thought was flat?

Suddenly the world was ending. My normally smooth-riding Bug seemed to be riding extremely roughly. (I don't know, maybe it was just the sparks flying through my window into my face that magnified the effect.) Although the Bug did seem to want to pull toward the turn lane, I was still not extremely worried.

I didn't get extremely worried until I waved to my left front tire, which was by then about five feet to my left and picking up speed. I still get a strange feeling about that one, not to mention the 10 or 12 cars traveling north making acrobatic moves to avoid the rubber missile.

"Focus! Focus!, my brain shouted as I cruised to a smooth

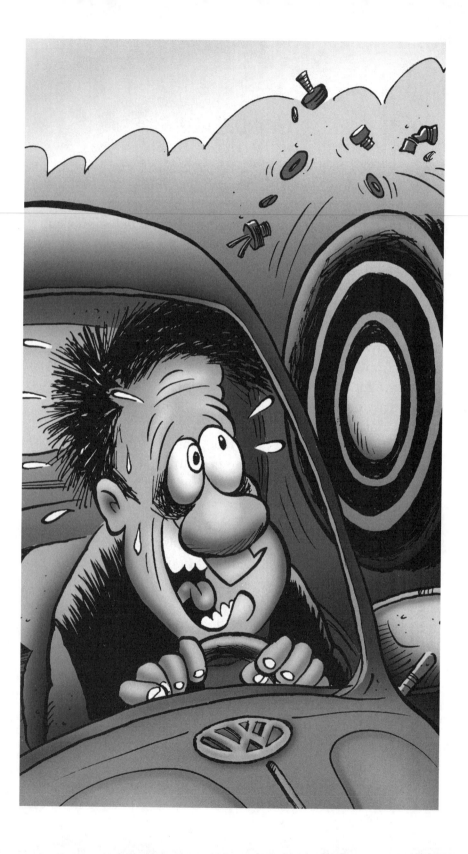

landing in the turn lane of a five-lane major thoroughfare. After collecting my thoughts (and changing underwear) I ran across the eastern two lanes of traffic into a real estate office. Cockily, I showed off my new AAA card and called for a tow. It would be at least a half hour, I was informed. No problem, that would give me plenty of time to track down my absent left wheel.

So down the strip I meandered, every now and then gazing back at my suddenly forlorn Bug sitting in the middle of traffic. Excuse me, did you see a tire pass this way, I asked every pedestrian I encountered while making my way south. What strange looks I received. Eventually, a helpful soul pointed to a small rundown hotel within distance. Things were looking up I thought, as I galloped to the hotel. I walked through the gate to the swimming pool, where I found a group of swimmers and sunbathers dazed by an uncontrollable round intruder. It seemed my errant tire hadn't bothered to use the gate and had instead rolled over it and entered the pool in a rather disruptive fashion. (And without even yelling, "Cannonball!")

Realizing the uncertainty of my predicament, I foolishly grinned (which I seemed to be doing more and more of) and fished my tire out of the pool. Thanking everyone within thanking distance, I gathered my tire under my arm and made my way back to the AAA rendezvous point.

A tow truck took my beloved Super Beetle to the nearest gas station for a week of rehabilitation. And I had a vacation I will always remember and cherish.

Jeff Eckerle

RUBBER BAND MAN

I was traveling home from college in my Bug when my accelerator got stuck because the cable was frayed. I used to be able to just tap the accelerator pedal to let it come out. But this time, as I was going along, each time I tapped it, it stuck. I was going along in the middle of nowhere in Pennsylvania with my accelerator pedal stuck to the floor.

When I started going too fast I finally pulled over. I thought, "What am I going to do? I'm in the middle of nowhere."

I studied the engine compartment and I figured out that if a spring in the back was a little bit stronger, it would make the cable come back and the accelerator pedal come up.

I didn't have an extra spring but I did have a rubber band. With nothing to lose, I wrapped it around next to the spring, and that got me home a couple of hours later. How many cars can be fixed with a rubber band?

Jim Tuohy

BEETLE JUICE

Growing up in the country, I counted on my 1963 Beetle to take me everywhere. My parents' home was about 10 miles from "civilization" in any direction. "Civilization", for our purposes here, will be defined as food, fuel and shelter. I'll never forget one particular evening when my Bug rescued me from sure disaster.

I had been to the high school football game. It was in December, with six inches of snow on the ground and colder than the proverbial well digger's posterior in the Klondike. There was a party after the game, about 25 miles from home. Suffice to say, the game was wild and so was the party. When I realized the time, I was already about 45 minutes past my curfew. I quickly excused myself, jumped in the car and sped away. (OK, I putt-putted away — it was, after all, a 1200 cc, 40 hp VW).

It may be interesting to note that '63 was the first year the VW Beetle had a gas gauge in the dash. Prior to that, one waited for the car to sputter out of gas, and then quickly engaged the "reserve" lever on the driver's side floorboard. I only mention this as a partial excuse for what was about to occur. You see, I was accustomed to driving pre-'63s, and when I knew I was low on fuel, I'd simply wait for the sputter, flip the lever, and be on my way.

Well, on this particular night, the car sputtered, I reached for the reserve tank lever, and there was none. I glanced at the gas gauge — dead empty! I coasted to a stop on the side of a deserted county road. I was still five miles from home and five miles from civilization. It was about 1 a.m., and there probably wouldn't be any traffic until the world started off for work in the morning — at least five more hours. Walking was out of the question, as I was wearing tennis shoes and the snow was six inches deep. What could I do? (Keep in mind, during my high school days, the cellular phone was still a gleam in some inventor's eye)

I mentally inventoried the contents of the trunk. There was nothing but the spare tire, jack, jack handle, jumper cables (don't drive a six-volt VW in the winter without 'em), small toolbox, and oh yeah, remnants of the party — two bottles of 100 proof vodka! It also was about a half-gallon of (dare I even think it) fuel.

I popped the hood, lifted the handle with one hand while pushing toward the windshield with the other in order to clear the bumper (they were all that way after they'd been hit once in the front end), opened the gas cap, and glug, glug, glug! I hopped in the car, turned the ignition key all the way. "Rrr, rrr, rrr, rrr, rrr." I turned the key off, then on again, "Rrr, Rrr, rrr, vroooom!" I couldn't believe it! It not only ran on vodka, it loved the stuff! It ran like a scalded dog all the way home!

Jeff Fortenbery

AN ENEMA TUBE BY ANY OTHER NAME
WOULD DELIVER BUG FUEL JUST THE SAME

My Volkswagen Beetle was the car that I drove every day, to the hospital and to the office where I had an ob/gyn practice. I wanted a VW for the ease of parking at the hospital, and for getting around in all kinds of weather with no trouble. A couple of my friends had them, too, and were very high on them.

Mine was a '62; I bought it in late '61. That was the year the Beetle went from 36 horsepower to 40 horsepower. My VW was green, like the color of a Granny Smith apple. I paid $1,800 for it. It was the deluxe one.

I remember the time I had just finished delivering a baby at roughly 1 or 1:30 in the morning, and I'd had a phone call from a patient who was having some kind of problem. The family only lived a few blocks from the hospital, and I said I would stop by and see her — which we did a lot in those days.

I drove out of the parking lot and had gone maybe a block or so, and the car started missing, going "chug, chug, chug." It would run a little bit and miss a little bit. So I stopped but I didn't turn off the engine. I opened the hood and gasoline just poured out. Every time the engine would turn over it would spurt gas.

I realized the problem was that a hose had developed a hole in it. So I turned the engine off and reached down to check. The rubber tubing was just like a piece of wet macaroni. It kept breaking off. I took a piece of it, and thought, it's 1:30 in the morning. Where in the world am I going to find something like this? And I was a little anxious to go check on my patient.

So I walked back to the hospital and went back to the delivery room, where we had quite a collection of rubber tubing. There was some enema tubing, we also called it rectal tubing, made of a little heavier rubber, and it was the same diameter that I needed. So I just took a piece of it, and carried it back to the car. I cut a chunk of it off and fitted it on the fuel pump and over to the carburetor and the thing started right up and ran.

That VW was still running on that same tube when I got rid of it in 1975.

Edward Honey

ONE CHAR-BROILED THING — TO GO

About 1992, one of my brothers owned a '74 VW Thing. Mark had fixed it up really nice and it ran great. But one thing that always bothered him was if we reached over 55 mph the whole car would shake violently. Another problem was the poor speed. My brother's was a lot slower than most. It just could not handle going up hills well at all.

Mark sold the VW Thing to our brother, Dan. One day, however, he borrowed it for the day. Mark, being the know-it-all of VWs, said the fuel filter needed changing and took it upon himself to do so without Dan's knowledge. I remember looking at the one Mark had swapped and it didn't look overly in need of a change. But heck, I was only a teenager at the time and didn't know much about cars yet.

For lunch we went to the local Burger King. We were at the window waiting for our order when all of a sudden there was a huge explosion. Mark and I looked at each other in shock. Then, out of the corner of our eyes, we saw smoke pouring into the car and a huge wall of fire on the outside of the closed convertible rear window. Apparently "somebody" hadn't hooked up the fuel filter correctly and we had ignition!

I slid out of the VW while Mark somehow squeezed in between it and the drive-thru window and scampered across the hood to safety. Although it's not unusual to see charred vehicles on the sides of Los Angeles freeways it is unusual to see them ahead of you in the drive-thru lane, so the people in line behind us began feverishly trying to back up! The whole back end of the car was on fire and I could see the nice three-year-old forest green paint bubbling from the heat and flames and charring to a sooty black.

My brother couldn't do a thing except watch the car burn. Luckily, the Burger King manager gave us a fire extinguisher before any other damage could have been done. Within a matter of minutes the fire trucks arrived and pulled the Thing out to the parking lot and checked it for us to make sure it was OK.

Black smoke from the fire had seared the side of the building and left soot on the stucco wall. To top it off, the bushes next to the building burned to ash, leaving a five-foot area without any shrubs at all.

I still drive by that Burger King and see they tried their best to scrub the soot off the building but it's still there — along with patch of bushes that never grew back Almost every day I am reminded of that experience. The Thing still runs to this day, though — charred paint and all.

Dave Andrews

AND THIS ONE IS OUT OF THE PARK

My husband and I played softball together. It was 1972 and our team was playing at a new field in a rural area. He and I headed to the field in the daylight but when the time came to head home after the game and a couple of beers, it was dark and the road looked a lot different.

I was driving our old Bug with the barely functional six-volt electrical system. The headlights enabled you to see a whole two feet ahead, so I wasn't actually where I thought I should be. This became even more clear when, at about 35 miles per hour, we careened off the road and into a cornfield two or three feet lower than the pavement.

"Dammit, turn the lights out, I don't want anybody to see us!" my husband said when we finally landed. He was so embarrassed, but I thought it was funny. All I could think about was how in the heck we were going to get out of there if nobody knew where we were.

Fortunately, a carload of kids that also had been coming from the ballfield saw what happened. They stopped, but were kind of afraid to approach our Bug, not knowing what they were going to find inside. Finally the only brave one in the group made his way toward us in the dark and shouted "Hey, anybody inside?" We had to admit to my slight miscalculation of the road.

Upon confirming that we weren't dead or mangled, the less-brave members of the group came down into the field. Together they were able to actually boost the Bug back up onto the road. Since we weren't hurt the accident turned out to be just one of those fun times...something to remember.

Terri Keller

BY THE SEAT OF MY PANTS

It was a gray, fall day. My friend Tom and I, both in our late teens and with apparently nothing better to do, set out on a road trip — something we were known to do with little provocation. We would head south and go camping.

We both had '74 Super Beetles, nearly identical except for one detail. Mine was reliable. For reasons beyond logical explanation, we decided to take his for our weekend excursion.

Tom's engine sounded strong and healthy as we made our way down I-75 from our homes near Cincinnati and headed south. Suddenly, about 10 miles north of the nearest town, that "all's right with the world" feeling ended. One moment we were sailing along at about 60 mph, the next moment we simply weren't. We were losing speed fast.

The motor was running but the throttle wasn't responding. We both knew these symptoms. Tom and I looked at one another and in a flurry of cursing shouted, "Throttle cable!" That's something you can't readily repair but can easily replace if you have a spare. Maybe it was rebellion against our conservative upbringing, but Tom and I liked to live on danger's edge. We rarely carried a spare of anything. This was about as rebellious as we got.

We got out and confirmed our diagnosis. Damn! We were right. The big question, "Now what?"

We were in the middle of nowhere, no houses within sight and it was beginning to get dark. I wasn't exactly fond of the idea of hitching a ride with the first homicidal psychopath that pulled over and offered a ride to wherever we wanted to go. It was time to think.

Somewhat in disgust, I sat on the back bumper. I leaned back to lay against the fender when — "plop" — I made an important discovery. My bony butt fit tightly between the fender and the shock-absorbing bumper. Through some positioning and experimentation I further discovered that if I held onto the open deck lid with my right hand, I could manipulate the throttle with my left. The wheels of my mind were turning. Maybe this could work.

We agreed that I would operate the throttle and yell "shift" at the appropriate times. We would prudently proceed down the safety lane at a slow speed until we hit civilization. Our plan was to find a place to buy the replacement part and either proceed on or spend the night.

As we made our way along, we both became fairly comfortable with this arrangement. One would even say we actually got pretty good at it. This, however, was not the time to revel in our ingenuity because the sky was getting darker. I'll never forget the look of disbelief on Tom's face when I yelled, "Let's go for it, merge!" In perfect sync, we upshifted and made our way up to 60 mph and merged into the right lane. Maybe it was the wind or the close-up look at moving pavement but at this point, I was beginning to question the wisdom of my suggestion to merge. Maybe it was the fact that the only thing between me and eternity was the bumper that Tom reattached after the last paint job.

Hey, wait. Check it out. Suddenly I'm a celebrity. People are honking and waving. The looks on the faces of the other motorists ranged from laughter to utter horror.

At last, we approached an exit for a small town. Still caught up in my instant fame among our fellow motorists, I noticed the one that seemed to take the most active interest in our situation was the officer now positioning himself behind us. Big surprise: the lights went on. I wasn't about to suggest we try to lose him with me on the back bumper, so we pulled over.

At first he tried to be "Mr. By-the-Book Tough Guy". That didn't last. He assessed the situation and before long couldn't keep a straight face. After determining that we were not

completely insane, he expressed that his major concern was our safety. He knew of a parts store nearby. At the officer's suggestion, we resumed our team approach to driving and he escorted us through town like some slow-moving freak parade.

Fortunately, the store was less than a mile away and the part was in stock. We installed it in a half hour, continued onto our trip and swore we'd tell our parents that our weekend was uneventful.

Paul Klebahn

BACK FROM THE DEAD

I guess it was in the mid 1960s when I got a '57 Volkswagen with God knows how many miles on it, probably 100,000 or more. It was gold, and it was the body type that had the small oval window in the back. I think it was maybe the first year that had the electric turn signals instead of the little arm that flipped up on the side of the car.

The body was in really bad shape. It had a lot of rust and you could see the pavement through the holes in the floorboards. When it rained the spray would come flying up from the floor so I had to keep wiping my glasses as I drove. But it ran. It really ran.

After I had it for about two years I had the engine rebuilt. Everything was going fine until I drove down to New Orleans to visit a friend.

On my way back to St. Louis, somewhere in Louisiana, I was struck from behind by a car going about 35 mph. I was stopped at a traffic light and the impact slammed me into the car in front of me.

I wasn't hurt, but when I got out to inspect the damage, I noticed that my car was about 10 inches shorter and six inches taller than it was before.

Upon checking the damage to the engine, I found that the collision had jammed the back bumper into the engine cover. Also, the front bumper was pushed into the trunk. So I couldn't open either the trunk or the engine cover anymore.

I drove it that way for a few months until I realized it was time to get rid of the car.

I called an auto wrecker and offered to sell him the car for its scrap metal value. He gave me $75 which seemed fair and I said goodbye to the car.

About two weeks later I was walking down the street when I

saw my old car go by. The wrecker had sold it to someone else. The car just would not die. I'm sure someone is driving it even now.

Harold Ramis
Actor/Writer/Director

ON THE EDGE

Sometime in the mid Eighties, I was tooling around the town where I went to college in my bright yellow 1968 Beetle. I had bought it after high school graduation in 1980 and shortly thereafter, had it painted by a friend in his back yard for $75. This after spending countless hours scraping off the yellow paint that was on it when I bought it. Yellow, latex house paint, applied with a brush. On a hot summer South Carolina day, you could just nick a spot with a key and then peel back a pretty good sized rubbery sheet. But with "real" paint on it, it looked OK and was serving me well as a classic college car.

One day I collided with a white Toyota. Once it was clear that no one was hurt, I climbed outside to assess the damage. The whole left rear fender of my Beetle was collapsed onto the now-airless tire. Trying to convince myself that it wasn't that bad, I jumped back in the car, started it, put it in gear and tried to limp it out of the middle of the road. When I let the clutch out, there was a whirring sound and a slight grinding, but the car moved nary an inch. I had it towed to Howard's VW repair business about five miles from school.

While I had done some tune-up stuff myself, I had enlisted Howard's services before for a few odd repairs. His place is along a rolling road in green foothills of the Smokey Mountains. You might easily pass it save for the little Beetle-shaped sign that hung from the bottom of the mailbox. He had a very clean looking white '67 Beetle of his own that took shelter nearby.

Howard explained that the force of impact had traveled down the axle and destroyed the differential in the transmission. He said he could put a used transmission in there for $200, and that it would take a couple weeks. He said I needed to get him another tire; he had another rim he could sell me. I asked him about the fender to which he quickly replied that he didn't do body work. I told him that I just needed to be able to drive the car and that I could get the taillight and all working again.

"Well, you know, I have a cousin coming to visit this weekend," Howard told me. "I think he likes to mess around with these things a bit. I'll see what he can do."

Two weeks later the car was ready, but Howard said there was a problem.

"It howls." he said.

"It what?"

"It howls, the transmission roars. Must be worn out", he said. "You can drive it, but it is loud."

He insisted that I bring the car back when he got another transmission and he would replace it free of charge. I asked about the fender.

"Oh yeah, Carl had quite a time with that one, but we got it fixed", he said. "Hope you don't mind blue. It was all we had".

My yellow car with a blue fender was actually better than I expected, but I decided stop at the local hardware store on the way home and pick up a couple cans of yellow spray paint.

Once I got on the road, I understood what "howl" meant. Windows up, windows down, radio on, it didn't matter. All you heard was a deafening noise from the rear end of the car. I started noticing people turning and looking at my car.

A few weeks later, Howard called to tell me that he had another transmission and that I should bring my car back. I was glad because the howling was starting to give me headaches. Howard told me that he had just bought a '70 Beetle "for parts" from a fella for a few hundred dollars and that to his surprise, it had a swing axle transmission (they were replaced by IRS trannies in '69 in the U.S. market).

Howard and I strolled to the back part of his property, the part that looked like a small junkyard. I didn't see anything that looked driveable but as I walked by a faded yellow Beetle, Howard said "here we go" and yanked open the door.

I'm still not sure exactly what about this car made it look undriveable. The tires were low on air and the windows were filthy. Howard plopped into the driver's seat and the car groaned a bit. I opened the passenger door and upon seeing almost a good square foot of the green grass below the car in front of the passenger seat, opted not to sit down until I received further instructions. I thought maybe he would start it and then let me drive it. There was some grass visible under his feet too, as he furiously pumped the gas pedal. He turned the key and the engine wheezed. Just as the cranking speed slowly waned away to what seemed like the "that's it, battery's dead" sound Howard flailed even faster on the gas pedal. There was a pop, a sputter and with a puff of gray smoke, the engine started up.

I sat down gently in the wet seat. It seemed to give and leaned to the right a bit. I looked down and carefully found enough solid metal on the floor to rest my feet. The whole car smelled like and old wet blanket.

We rolled slowly down the grassy lawn, onto the driveway and out onto the road. As we got going, Howard pressed the brake pedal and it went all the way to the floor. He peered intently down the road. He pumped the brake pedal a couple more times, but each time it touched the back of the fire wall with a metallic thud. Suddenly, there was a groan and the sound of metal tearing, and my seat tilted toward the right some more, the backrest was now touching the door. I looked down and could see a bit more if the road whizzing past. Howard still kept his businesslike look, and we hit third. He finally broke his silence, took his hand off the gear shift and said "See?"

"Great!" I said. "Perfect." I could now feel the strange sensation of wind blowing up between my legs, and the car was starting that rhythmic bounce of a vehicle on less-than-balanced tires. As the bouncing intensified the front part of my seat jolted forward as now the front edge of the seat rails tore away from the floor. I grabbed the "Jesus handle" on the dash and pressed

hard with my feet. I prayed that they wouldn't tear through the
floor as I had the feeling that if I lifted them up and let go of the
dash, the whole seat would rotate forward and down, the seat
and I would do a header onto the highway and I would get a
nice look at my new tranny as the back end of the car passed
over me.

Just as I was about to register a concern with Howard about
my seating, he slammed the car into fourth and pressed the gas
pedal to the floor. Without taking his eyes off the road, he
shouted as we both now bounced violently along, "See! This is
where most of them go bad. They jump out under load in fourth.
This one is fine!" I nodded and looked up. We were going a tad
over 50 mph and there was a sharp turn coming up. I wondered
whether Howard had remembered the results of the brake pedal
test I had witnessed just moments earlier. "Awright then," he
said as he got off the gas and slipped the car into neutral. "Grab
the wheel." I stared at him, puzzled. "Right here!" he said, a
little more urgently pointing the right side of the steering wheel
but never taking his gaze off the road.

The calmness of his voice led me to believe that he knew
what he was doing. I gingerly lifted my left hand off the Jesus
handle and grabbed the outer edge of the steering wheel. Still
without taking his eyes of the road, and the upcoming curve,
Howard took both hands off the steering wheel, reached down
and grabbed the emergency brake handle. He pulled it up slowly
but firmly. In hindsight, my diagnosis of this car is that in
addition to its other shortcomings, only one emergency brake
cable must have been intact because as the brakes (er, "brake")
engaged the car lurched toward the embankment on the right.
Instinctively, I grabbed the wheel with my other hand and
shoved it to the left. As I did so, the seat violently fell even
more forward and I think my right shoulder hitting the dash was
all that kept me from exiting the vehicle without use of either
door. I saw myself as child, running through a sprinkler in our

front yard back in Virginia. My life was flashing through my mind...

Howard didn't take his gaze off the road or both hands off the emergency brake handle until we had come to a full stop. He looked over at me and started to comment on the performance of the transmission, but changed his topic when he saw my whitened face. "See? Damn nice tra.... oh, I guess that seat's about to finally let go, huh?" Yeah, I think that would be a safe statement.

Howard put the car in first, checked for traffic, made a careful U-turn and started heading back up the road to his shop. "Well there ya go. I think it'll work for ya nice, and it doesn't make noise either."

After a brief pause, I said "Yep, it is a LOT quieter than that other one. But I think I heard some gear noise in second. Do you mind driving all the way back in second so I can listen?"

I pressed my feet down harder and the seat groaned back at me.

John S. Henry

SALESMAN ON THE HOT SEAT

I used to use my '74 Beetle to go on sales calls when I worked as a representative for a large payroll and data processing services firm. It was my mobile office and the area behind the back seat served as my file cabinet where I kept order forms and brochures.

One day I was working with a potential client and had to go out to the Bug to get another form. As usual, I got in the passenger door and put my knee on the back seat to reach my materials. This time however, the springs from the seats made contact with the battery and set the seat ablaze.

Luck was with me that day. Frantic and red-faced, I was able to pull the flaming seat out before the whole car went up. My potential client saw everything from the window and ran out to help. Together, we were able to put out the fire in a matter of moments.

Once things were under control and I went back to my sales pitch, the guy said the least he could do was give me an order after all of this happened.

Although I never repeated it, I was glad to add this closing technique to my sales repertoire.

Bill Berckman

EASY SLIDER

In the early 1970s I was driving my '59 Bug down a rural
highway when I came upon some road construction. The only
way around was through a field. The detour wasn't very long,
not much more than just a dirt path down a mild slope and then
back up again. I could see the other side several hundred yards
away. It had been raining steadily for several days but being
young and foolish I didn't think much of it. I started down the
detour slowly and got to the bottom of the slope when the
ground started getting soft and slick. Getting more foolish by
the minute I thought this was great fun, so I floored it. The rear
wheels started spinning and the Bug promptly sank up to the
floor boards. All forward, backward and sideways motion
quickly came to a halt. All I could do was spin the tires and
keep on sinking.

When I got out to walk up to the highway to look for help, I
took one step and sank halfway to my knees in the mud. I took
another step and lost both of my shoes in the sludge. I took one
more step and fell on my butt. This was no longer fun but I
didn't think it could get much worse. Wrong!

I heard the sound of the motorcycles long before they came
over the hill. As I stood in the mud, a dozen or so "bikers"
approached.They looked rough and they looked mean. It was
pretty obvious that they had been out partying and having a
good time. It didn't take them long to spot me and my Bug
stuck in the mud at the bottom of the hill. As they stared and
laughed at me I started getting more then a little nervous. I was
a teenager and had seen all of the biker movies of the Sixties. I
knew I was in some deep doo-doo.

After the bikers had their laugh they started walking toward
me. Some of them slipped and cursed the mud. My young
nerves were shot. I started to contemplate begging for my life.

Once they got down the hill, they just kind of stared at me. One of them told me to "start walkin'" and pointed to the top of the hill. I didn't argue. I started in the direction he had pointed as fast as I could, slipping and sliding.

As I looked back from a relatively safe distance, I saw them surround my poor Bug and lift it straight out of the mud. Then they proceeded to carry it most of the way back up the hill until they hit some solid ground. They set it down and one of them got in and backed it the rest of the way up the hill to where I was. All through this they were just laughing and having a good time. Afterward they didn't say much, just cleaned a little of the mud off their boots, got on their bikes and roared back the way they came.

I was so dumbfounded I couldn't speak. I didn't even get a chance to thank them for the help, the kindness and most importantly for letting me live.

Randy Meiner

LIKE A SHIP WITHOUT A RUDDER

My Beetle is over 30 years old. It was a gift from my Dad after high school graduation. One of my fondest memories came when we were living in Texas and I got caught in a sudden, blinding Texas rainstorm, the kind where your windshield wipers don't even do any good.

I was traveling beneath a freeway overpass when my Bug got caught in the waist-deep water that had accumulated there. People have always said that VWs could float because their undersides were sealed, and this was my chance to find out if that was true. Sure enough, the car started floating uncontrollably. It was an eerie feeling! It was like trying to navigate without a rudder. I was afraid I was going to float into another car and damage something so I hung out the window waving for people to get out of my way. The ordeal seemed like it took an eternity.

Eventually, I bobbed straight through the freeway intersection. Despite that episode, I was the only one of the four kids in my family to keep my Bug. At first I didn't want to but I could never get rid of it. Now I'm glad I didn't.

Donna Badger

BLINDED BY THE LIGHTER

I had only had my Bug for a short while when I was elected to drive on a night out on the town with the girls. We enjoyed some adult refreshments before we left.

Everyone liked my cute little car with the pictures on the knobs, plenty of room for five and a good AM radio. After a couple of blocks and a stop at an intersection I realized that I was driving without my headlights on. A couple more blocks and another stop sign, and I realized once more that my lights were not on. I started having second thoughts about my ability to drive but with all of the talking and laughter in the car I did not mention this to my passengers.

The next stop I made was at a traffic light. NO HEADLIGHTS. I quietly reached for the headlight button (as I thought I had done twice before) when my passenger looked at me and said, "Doesn't your cigarette lighter work?"

Phyllis Hartman

REALLY HEAVY, MAN

For my 1975 post-college entry into the car world I
purchased a '65 VW Bug from the snot-nosed, next-door
neighbor kid, who had rejuvenated it as a junior high shop
project. I also dutifully purchased a cheap repair manual, intent
on learning mechanics as an adjunct to being a poor but honest
professional pottery maker.

Now one thing about pottery is that in dealing with clay,
we're talking really heavy, man. Clay is typically purchased by
the ton, and the finished work is delightful, but not light.
Eventually I broke down and got a pickup, but first I needed to
earn the money for that option. So I would haul clay materials,
roughly 750 pounds at a time, in my Bug. To go to art fairs I
would haul all the shelves on the roof, and cram the inside full
of pottery. This heaviness property of pottery was to cause me
grief several times.

It was on the way to a big art fair that I heard a thunk and
felt a loss of power. How can you feel a loss of power in a 40
hp Volkswagen? I assure you, it is possible. Suddenly my top
speed was 40, instead of 62. Needing to get to the fair, I kept
going. After the fair, I drove it home. My repair manual
recommended a compression check, and one of the pistons
showed no pressure. It also recommended shining in a
flashlight, and looking at it while cranking the engine. I did this,
and saw the end of the piston stationary at the end of the
cylinder.

For those of you who are seriously mechanically challenged,
like me, the piston is like a big roundish chunk of aluminum
which goes back and forth at odd moments in the close confines
of its friendly cylinder. It is connected to its buddy, the rod,
which hooks into a bunch of other complicated gadgets.
Imagine if your head was stuck in a sewer pipe, going up and

down. In this instance your neck would be the equivalent of the rod. So when I took the engine apart, the piston had split in half, dutifully leaving the part connected to the rod in place, still dutifully going up and down the cylinder, so that I could get where I needed to, instead of "throwing a rod." In our illustration, this is your baseball cap sticking further in the sewer pipe, leaving your head still connected to your neck, free to continue on its merry way.

A year or so later, my wife and I were moving from Minnesota to Oregon. We had obtained the certified Okie pickup truck, with all our earthly possessions in the back. We decided to tow our VW as a trailer, filled with stuff, and got the local blacksmith to make a sturdy steel tube and chain arrangement to hook onto the VW bumper. On the day we left, somehow one of us managed to leave the Bug securely in first gear. (For the purpose of marital reconciliation, the perpetrator shall remain anonymous). Twenty miles later, some telltale smoke alerted us to the fact that the rear tires had pretty much quit turning. In fact, the transmission held and the engine "threw a rod." This was bad, but not terrible. After all, a friend had donated a used VW engine and we had it along in back of the truck. So we continued on our way.

The VW would wobble back and forth a bit as we cruised along, steadily straining at the bit, one might say. The technical term for this is metal fatigue. Two hundred miles into the journey, we accelerated away from a stop light in Fargo, North Dakota and the VW stayed behind. The bumper had become disconnected. We had not yet heard the chorus of voices telling us, "you can't tow a Beetle by the bumper." Incidentally, this bumper was the classic, in-your-face bumper, not the namby pamby metal Band-Aid strip which replaced it in later models. When it broke off, two tough strips of metal remained facing forward. We secured the chains to these, and continued.

We ended up in Chelan, Washington, still poor and honest,

and still doing art fairs with the VW Bug. (I think the truck had developed a brake problem, as in, no brakes). We had a streak of luck, and qualified for an art fair run for well-to-do area residents. The only thing between us and financial success was McNeil Canyon. At the bottom was the Columbia River. To get to the top was to climb over 2,000 feet at a steep rate of ascent. The car was packed almost to the running boards with pots and the roof loaded with display shelving.

You all know the unique whine of the VW engine — I believe it is "The Song of the Rings" or "Nibelungen" or something. By the time I crested the canyon, the engine was making a new variation on the song. It was something like "The Death Throes of the Valkyrie." Once again, I Needed to Get There. And the car kept going. And I Needed to Get Home. And the car kept going. We made big money from the art fair, and set off for Spokane to buy a new car.

Have you ever heard of the Judas Cows that led the cattle yearly on the Texas Trails to the rail yards (and a future of slaughterhouses)? They got to return to lead other cows on their death march. Our VW was Not That Sort of Animal. It threw a rod on the way to our trading it in. Even its death was graceful, though. It died rolling down a hill, and stopped by a potato warehouse, from whence we called a wrecker. We sold it to the wrecker driver for enough to buy bus tickets to Spokane, and the he even drove us to the bus station. The Beetle era was ending, although I don't doubt that our VW was rejuvenated several times before its true final rest. The Beetles were so interchangeable, you know. Kind of the epitome of reinCARnation....

Brad Sondahl

CHAPTER FIVE

CUPID HAS THE KEY

Bug tales of love

THE GREATEST GIFT OF ALL

My first car was a 1964 VW. It was my freedom and my membership into the right club. The Bug was the first automotive symbol for young, hip and politically correct. We were proud drivers. We honked when we passed other VWs on the road. We were cool.

The only thing I would have changed about my Bug was the color. I wanted it in khaki. The dealer didn't have it. For a while, I thought about repainting the car, but never did.

In '75 I bought my second VW Bug — this time a bright red convertible. I still couldn't get khaki. Nineteen years and six months later, I sold that car. My life had changed. I got married to a man who has a passion for antiquing, had two children, got a dog and traded up to a roomier, family-friendly car. It made perfect sense, but silently I pined for a khaki VW Bug.

One night, early this past summer, my husband came home and called me to come outside. You guessed it. Hidden behind our four-wheel-drive sat a 70 khaki VW Bug, complete with Bug mats on the floor and a rainbow decal on the back window.

I screamed. I hugged him. I got in the car and drove and drove and I smiled. I had my car. But more important, I had received the most loving gift. Without a word from me, my husband had heard what I had been asking for. In the driveway, I had a total affirmation that the man I loved really knew me. It was proof that to be the person I have always wanted to be, I never had to trade in who I really am.

Rochelle Udell
Editor-in-Chief, Self magazine

CALIMANZI

I must confess, I acquired my first Bug through a process of panic, then compromise. I had been fond of Volkswagens most of my life. One of my earliest memories was driving through the mountains of North Carolina in a Bug that belonged to friends of the family. As we came to a tunnel a Volkswagen bus came out. The honking and waving they exchanged was not something that went on between my parents and other Pontiac owners.

By 1973 I was an 18-year-old senior in high school. The love of VWs was taking a back seat to the yearning for a cool set of wheels. My father and I had agreed it was time to look for my first car. I had found a '68 Mustang that was "rednecked" to the hilt. The look in my father's eyes made his thoughts quite audible. "Why don't we go ahead and cancel the family insurance. It will happen after his first four tickets." This obviously was not where his money would be spent.

His idea of the perfect car for a teenage male was a four-door, four-cylinder Chevy Nova with an automatic transmission. I didn't realize they made Novas that boring until he said he had a friend in the car business looking for just such a monster. I believe my eyes were also speaking volumes. "Why not just get me some pants I can pull up to my chest and a pocket protector. Do members of the football team still beat up nerds in college?"

Desperate not to be a role model for "Revenge of the Nerds XXXIV" I volunteered to purchase my own first car. That instantly ruled out most muscle cars, but it kept me out of a rolling "kick me" button, too.

After great searching, we found a '66 Beetle that belonged to a missionary studying at the Baptist seminary in Louisville. She had named the car "Calimanzi" after a fruit in the Philippines. She was using it to commute between Boston and Louisville. This was obviously a car with a history and some character.

Instead of wax she protected the paint with "crazy daisy" decals.

Little did this poor, innocent car know the changes it was about to experience. Calimanzi was dark green under the daisies. In those days I spent a great deal of time with two brothers whose family attended our church. One drove a dark green '67 Bug. The other drove his girlfriend's '65 dark green Bug. We looked like a parade after church on Sundays. Actually, we were a parade. The owner of the '67 talked me into combining our interiors. His was black. Mine was white. So in honor of the court-ordered busing in our town, and as a salute to racial harmony, we traded passenger seats and back seat bottoms. I don't know if that would be considered politically correct or incorrect. Then it was just fun. Why else own a Bug?

My most memorable evening with Calimanzi happened when I was at college. A popular campus "parking" area was atop a steep hill near the married students' apartments. My boss was among the residents there. One night I was in the back seat with a willing participant (fortunately, she was not a tall lass). We were in various stages of undress. With timing that could be called embarrassing as well as divine intervention, the emergency brake malfunctioned. I hadn't turned the wheels toward the curb so away we went. While the young lady and I were dreaming of someday living in married housing, this was not how we planned to get in.

I'm not certain how I got into the front seat and stopped poor Calimanzi. The young lady and I broke up several times before calling it quits for real. Calimanzi was traded but its British replacement was a failure. I returned to the VW fold. I have since owned more VWs than I care to admit, but none of these have made such bold efforts at keeping me on the straight and narrow. I believe when I seek cars for my own sons, I'll call missionaries first. I'm too young to be a grandfather.

Mark Turpin

UNREQUITED LOVE

In June of 1969, at the tender age of 19, I had a '63 VW Beetle. I also had a mad crush on a girl from Denver who I had met at a wedding in Cincinnati, my hometown.

We stayed in touch. She broke up with her boyfriend and invited me to visit her in Denver. At the time I was doing odd jobs at a local radio station — answering the request line, doing some announcing work and helping out in the newsroom.

I got off the air on at 9 p.m. one Sunday, went directly into a gas station, charged two new front tires for my Beetle and, with a week off, headed out for Denver.

Driving non-stop for 19 hours I finally arrived to discover that my friend wanted to be just that and nothing more.

Suffice to say, I was a bit crushed — and had a longing that would go unrequited. I also was looking at a long drive home.

The young lady in question had a younger brother who needed a ride back to Cincinnati. Eureka! Someone to help with the driving!

Well, no, not actually. He couldn't drive a standard shift.

But I was desperate for sleep. So I put Junior in the driver's seat, worked the pedals and got him up to highway speed, then I'd nod.

I was interrupted every so often by my young companion either running out of gas (he didn't want to wake me) or because he had to downshift behind a semi and needed me to resurrect some momentum with my "leg over the hump" manipulation of the pedals. Some might suggest that was what I had in mind for his sister....

Nonetheless, it was a safe, if excruciating, trip home and I'm sure something similar has happened to another VW drivers over the years.

But here's hoping their love didn't go unanswered.

As for me, I'm back in love, with my white '79 Beetle convertible. I refer to it as my "poor-man's Porsche."

Dennis Janson

CHICK MAGNET

My prized possession is a baby blue 1971 Super Beetle that my parents bought for me. I love the car and nothing can compare to the looks I get when I go cruising in the summer with the windows down and the sun sparkling off the chrome. Peoples' eyes seem to become fixed on it as they think back to the time when they had their first VW — most likely their first car.

The absolute best thing about Beetles is the strange attraction women have to them. Numerous times girls have come up to my car and told me how much they love Bugs, and how they're so cute.

This attraction was proven to my father one day when I needed to use his car for school. Consequently, he was forced to drive my Bug to work. On the way home he stopped to get gas. While refueling, a young, very attractive blonde woman walked up to him and complimented him on how nice the car was. She told him how she just loved Beetles and asked if she could sit in it. Being the nice guy that he is, my Dad said he didn't have a problem with it. As she slid in, she kept saying how she loved it and asked how long he had owned it.

Upon telling her "it belongs to my son" she immediately got out and resumed what she was doing before she came over. I wonder if things would have been different if I'd been there!

Andrew J. Worrall

SWEET REVENGE

I was 16 in 1978. I had a few dates with a guy who drove a Volkswagen Beetle and was into photography. If he hadn't had those two traits — inextricably linked in my mind since he had one of his own photographs of a raccoon displayed on the passenger's side dashboard — I don't think I would remember him now.

Other girls dreamed about guys with more expensive sports cars but I wanted a guy with depth. This one's VW told me he knew how to have style on a low budget. I thought for sure we'd get married. I mean, we had at least three or four really fun dates.

But I was to learn a terrible lesson about boys: If they wanted to they could just STOP CALLING. After the fourth or fifth day (I gave it a while because answering machines, call waiting, etc. weren't commonly used) I realized that there would be no more rides in the Bug (literally, OK?).

I had to teach this guy a lesson. After all, I had years of dating ahead of me and letting him get away with this kind of behavior would set a dangerous precedent. My girlfriends and I had a job over the summer stuffing envelopes for a professional NFL team. While doing that job we found garbage bags full of Styrofoam packing peanuts. (Years later I wondered whether they had actually been discarded; we really thought they were trash at the time.) We held onto these figuring we'd find something fun to do with them.

The Saturday night after Mr. VW didn't call back we happened to be driving around town with these in the trunk. Nothing much was going on so we amused ourselves by driving by people's houses to see who was home and who wasn't. Luck would have it that he was home and the VW unlocked. In the summer night, under the light of the street lamp and with a great

sense of risk, we dumped all of the peanuts into the car. They just about made it up to the steering wheel. We all thought it looked really cute that way. But then we were just a bunch of girls and we didn't have to clean them out of there.

Epilogue: This was all done in good fun. I didn't continue any more of this delinquent behavior until I was well into adulthood.

Name Withheld Upon Request

WEDDED BLISS

I have always been in love with the Volkswagen Beetle. I have always made this fact very clear to others by the stickers and artwork on my car.

For me, it all started many years ago when my proud parents brought me home in their brand new 1974 Sun Bug. That was the metallic gold kind with a sunroof. This Beetle was their first new car as a married couple and I was their first baby. It seemed to go together rather well. A few months ago, my father told us a story that until then I had never heard.

It seems that whenever my parents would take their beloved Bug and son (I still don't know which order it should be) to the drive-in, I would just cry and cry. Until, that is, they would start up the car and make laps around the drive-in. Once I would fall asleep they could stop and watch the movie as long as they would keep the engine running! This was the only way they could get me to sleep. I thought this story was so cool, and no doubt another part of the reason why I'm a VW fan.

In December of 1996, while overlooking the beautiful city of Pittsburgh on top of Mount Washington, I asked my girlfriend to marry me. We used my brother's '67 VW microbus for our wedding-day transportation. Some months later, my new wife and I continued starting our new life together by buying a Beetle!

Josh Byler

GOING FULL CIRCLE

On the Fourth of July in 1966, Bev and I were traveling across the Pocono Mountains between her home in New Jersey, where we were planning our wedding, and Wilkes Barre, Pennsylvania, where we were attending school.

It was the summer before my senior year of college. Bev had just graduated from nursing school and was studying for her state board exams. We were happily planning the coming year. We had found an apartment and we were riding in our first car — a beautiful '63 Volkswagen Bug. Not a scratch marred its gray exterior. The canvas cover on the roof slid back to expose us to the summer sun and warm wind. Our suitcases and books were in the back seat because the Bug's trunk was filled with household items for our new apartment.

We took turns at the wheel and, on a rather deserted highway on top of those Pennsylvania hills, I was dozing and Bev was drinking in the joy of driving a stick shift on the open-road.

Suddenly, I was startled by a panicked yell from Bev and looked up to face a section of pavement that, at 50 mph, was coming up fast in front of us and as high as a curb! That summer was so hot that sections of concrete in the highway buckled. Some of them were several inches above normal! My reaction to her alarm was to brace myself for the inevitable crunching thump. I thought surely we would blow the tires! Bev turned the Bug sharply toward the right shoulder.

The Bug swerved and Bev dodged most of the slab but the left wheel hit it with such a force that the steering wheel spun completely to the right, out of her control. She and I both reacted by grabbing the wheel and turning hard to the left, trying to keep from flying into the thick, scrub-oak forest that lined the highway. However, we overcompensated and the Bug began to fishtail wildly. We found ourselves beginning to roll.

I was on my back sliding on the concrete highway with Bev in some position on top of me, then the car turned back onto its wheels and we were forced up through the opening of the roof to hip level, looking out over the front of the car. Bev took the brunt of the slam against the metal edge of the roof. We tumbled like that three times! I was sure that at some point we would be ejected and the Bug would crush us. Thank God, in an act of supreme mercy, no other cars were approaching us.

When we finally came to rest, we were upright partially into the woods off the left shoulder of the road. Bev found herself hanging over the driver's side of the windshield from the sunroof. I was on my back in the rear seat. Stunned and in shock, we spent some minutes before we realized that we were both alive, although unsure how badly each might be injured.

I could hear Bev calling to determine if I was still alive. Her cry was reassuring; I knew that she, thank God, had not been killed. We crawled out of the Bug and hugged each other, happy to have survived.

When we turned to survey our situation, we saw that our books and suitcases were strewn in the middle of the highway along the path of our roll. In the midst of it all were three of the Bug's windows and none were broken! No glass was broken! The Bug itself had been badly scratched from sliding but it did not appear lopsided and the tires were okay. It looked driveable, until I noticed it was sitting in a pool of oil. Then, before we could even consider what to do with our situation, a Pennsylvania state trooper arrived. I marveled at his timeliness then realized that, off the highway within a few hundred yards of our accident, there were a couple of house trailers with people standing by watching. Someone had called for help.

Bev was more seriously hurt than I, with bad bruises on her hips and abdomen. She was admitted to the hospital for a couple of days of observation because of the possibility of internal injuries. She recovered and carried our five children over the following 11 years. My injury was simply a badly scraped back that left a tattoo of sorts on one of my buttocks as a reminder of the adventure. The state police report credited the Bug for saving our lives.

Bev and I often look back on that accident and are ever thankful that, however we were forced back into the Bug with each roll, the action did save our lives. We loved that Bug, our first car, and look fondly at old pictures of us with it. Circumstances never permitted getting another one. We bought a VW bus in '68 because it was large enough to open a playpen and carry a potty. With our kids now grown, maybe we will go full circle in our retirement years, in another Bug.

Bev and Gene Decker

LIEGT MIR AM HERZEN*

The blue Beetle with snazzy custom wheels whipped into the parking lot. Out stepped a gorgeous young woman, new softball glove (price tag still attached) on her left hand and a pristine white ball in the other. As she hurried past our practice diamond toward another group, three (male) teammates and I paused in our warm-up tosses to admire the "view." One commented; "Gee, I wish she was here to try out for our team!"

Minutes later, she approached the four of us and quietly asked; "Is this the Columbus Ski Club team? A friend of mine said you needed more girls!" Thinking quickly for some way to impress her, I blurted out; "Hey, nice wheels!" In response I received a glowing smile and a very sweet "Why thank you!" We were married one year and four days later.

Brenda joined my company and we traveled together on business throughout the Midwest. In the late summer of '79 we stopped in Richmond, Indiana. There, in the City Hall parking lot, sat a beautifully restored Karmann Ghia convertible. She mooned and crooned over the car, wringing her hands and exclaiming: "Oh, isn't it beautiful? I've always wanted one of these!"

Years passed, children arrived and our vehicular needs changed. Brenda's blue Beetle was replaced by a Mustang hatchback, then a far more "practical" full-size Olds station wagon. (Dubbed the "Blue Beast", the "Tank" and several other unprintable titles by Brenda.)

One of my habits has always been to read the "Antique and Classic Cars" ads in the Sunday paper. During early 1987, one of them caught my eye. With a lot of help from Brenda's Dad, a retired Volkswagen master mechanic — plus a modest amount of money — my clandestine project began.

On Mother's Day, 1987, Brenda was led to the front porch

with her eyes closed. A set of keys was pressed softly into her hand. Her old dream had finally come true: a candy-apple red, '74 Ghia convertible gleamed proudly in the driveway. She'll never part with it.

I topped that momentous day 11 years later, though, when I surprised her with another red VW. This time it was a New Beetle, a modern version of the classic. It doesn't replace the precious Ghia; it just adds to our memories.

Jim Agan
* *"From the Heart"*

CHAPTER SIX

I SWEAR I'LL TURN THIS CAR AROUND...

Bug tales of family and children

LIKE A BIG TOY

In the past couple of years I have noticed a strange occurrence. While driving to and from work in my tomato red '67 Bug I'll often be distracted from my commuter reverie by little faces with big smiles. What catches my eye are fingers pointing, hands waving, and the obvious sense of excitement of children in the cars around me. It was during one of these experiences that I realized this truth: Kids love Beetles. I don't know why for sure, but I do have a theory. Kids can relate to Beetles. They're scaled in a child's size when it comes to cars, they're not overwhelming, but somewhat embracing and fun. They look like a big toy, and they're always smiling at you. (Look at the front of a Bug, and you'll see what I mean.) I think if a child could pick one car to be, it would be a Beetle.

There is a certain aura that surrounds these wonderful cars. Kids pick up on that immediately. It's a wonderful phenomenon. The Beetle seems to fill a generation gap. Grandparents can tell their grandchildren Beetle stories, or how their first car as a young married couple was a Beetle. The children can relate. I sometimes get uptight and frustrated waiting to move in traffic jam. Then I look over and see these innocent, curious kids and it somehow makes my drive a little more bearable. Their sense of awe and amusement energizes me. Suddenly, the lights are a little greener, the roads are a little shorter and my day is a little brighter. For that, I thank them.

Jeff Godby

CHRISTMAS 1966

It was December 1966 and the last-minute shopping rush
was on. Mom knew what had to be done and in the spirit of the
season, a full-scale, militaristic attack on a local Sears store was
launched.

No operation of this magnitude was complete without the
proper personnel or equipment. The additional personnel
consisted of my Grandmother/Head of Security. Being a toddler
at the time who just discovered the joys of making my parents
chase after me in public places, her job was to keep me
contained while Mom shopped. The equipment was my parents'
red 1961 Beetle with white leatherette interior — a vehicle that
wouldn't fail even on a bitterly cold day that was only expected
to get worse. There was nothing left to chance, and the
operation began.

After several hours of intense shopping, Mom was beaming
from the success of her venture and the precision in which it
was executed. There was nothing left on the list left to buy. A
quick stop at the grocery store on the way back and we would
be home. Mission accomplished.

We marched out into the cold and headed to the Beetle in
the parking lot. Upon reaching this welcome site, Mom put
down the packages at the passenger side and hastily reached for
her keys in order to get us out of the cold wind. Her expression
changed as she tried to gain entry. It was taking longer than
usual. She couldn't turn the key. "Hmm. It must be frozen," she
muttered as she rushed to the other side. There she went through
exactly the same motions but a bit more frantically. Apparently
our Beetle was voicing its displeasure about being taken out of
its warm garage by allowing its locks to freeze.

Mom didn't panic. She launched this operation and was
certain this was only a minor setback. With the packages in tow

she marched Grandma and me back into the relative warmth of the store lobby. There she would call my father at work and receive the words of wisdom that would get us back on track. Dad, being the MacGyver type, instructed her to heat her key with a match or blow in the key hole in order to warm the lock mechanism. He had done it time and again on other cars and it never failed to work.

Armed with this knowledge, Mom was unstoppable. The plans were drawn. Grandma would watch me and the packages in the lobby and Mom would fight the elements to break winter's grip on the Beetle's door locks. With matches in hand and a determined look face out she went to save this mission.

She reached the frozen Beetle and began to work like a master thief about to crack a safe. Over and over she heated the key with a match, blew in the key hole to try to unlock the car. Focused on the task at hand, Mom was unaffected by the cold wind and the passers by. That is, until she was tapped on the shoulder as she once again blew in the lock. She turned to find a tall man with car keys in hand and a smirk on his face. Immediately thinking she had been misidentified as a car thief, she launched into an explanation. His profound reply rings in Mom's ears to this day. He turned and pointed to our identical red '61 Beetle parked three spaces away and said "Maybe, lady, if you tried the right car it would work!" With Mom standing speechless, he put his key into the lock of the thought-to-be-frozen Beetle and opened the door. Now uncontrollably laughing, he expressed that it was an easy mistake and could have happened to anyone, but nothing could relieve her embarrassment. At that moment, she swore to herself that no one would ever find out about this incident.

Mom looked on the bright side, we had only lost a half hour and the mission was back on track. She headed back in to collect the packages, Grandma and me. We still had time to stop at the grocery store before heading home to relax and make

some attempt to forget the one embarrassing flaw in an
otherwise perfectly executed operation. She successfully got us
into our Beetle and off we went.

Any attempt Mom made to keep this "case of mistaken
Beetles" a secret were squashed in the grocery. Rounding the
corner of the second aisle she came face to face with her worst
nightmare. It was the same man whose laughing face was now
etched permanently into her memory. She had hoped to never
see him again but here he was and he recognized her. Delighted
that fate had brought them back together, he proceeded to retell
the story to his wife and anybody around that would listen. It
was a real hit. Now everyone knew.

Over the years, the story had become part of our family's
folklore and a fond memory of our beloved red Beetle. It was
told again and again at family gatherings. We never got the
other man's name, but I'm sure the story was told around his
dining room table for many years to comes as well. And of
course it was destined to became one of his family's favorite
memories of their little red Bug.

Paul Klebahn

ROCK-A-BYE

My (now-ex) wife Sharon and I had a beige 1960s-era Beetle back in '74. I bought it used because it was a good price and kind of a neat car for a daily driver. I froze in it, and for whatever reason whenever I made a left turn the horn beeped. But that wasn't any real problem.

When Sharon was nine months pregnant we were waiting and waiting for her to have the baby. Finally, I said "I'm going to take you for a drive in the Bug over the bumpiest road I can find as fast as I can go. Maybe that will work."

"No, you're not," she told me.

It was February, and cold out. But she finally agreed. She was so big she even had trouble getting into the car. But we took the drive just like I said and sure enough, she went into labor 18 hours later. Now that story is part of the family lore.

The funny thing was, our daughter, Heather, loved the ride in the car. When she wouldn't go to sleep we'd put her in a little basket we'd bought for her, put her in the back seat and drive around until she would fall asleep. It always worked.

I also remember when Heather was still less than a year old we went out to buy a Christmas tree. We found a pretty one that must have been 12 or 15 feet high. We didn't think our ceilings were 12 of 15 feet high, but we liked the tree and figured we'd saw off the bottom if we needed to once we got home. So I tied the tree on top of the VW with some string. There was one piece of string lashed down by the trunk and one piece lashed down by the engine. That tree flopped over the whole roof of the car, from end to end. When I drove uphill I was afraid it was going to slide off. The whole time I was driving I could see the string fraying. Finally we made it. It was a miracle!

We kept the car for three or four years and I liked it more and more. It broke my heart every time I had to have anything done to it. Finally I had to give it up because it needed a lot of engine work.

Even though Sharon and I split up she remembers our VW. She'd tell you these same stories. I'm sure we'll both remember them for a long time.

Ken Ashford

THE GHIA EFFECT

My mother was 19 years old in 1956 and about six months pregnant with me. She and my Dad drove to a VW dealer in North Hollywood with the sole intention of checking out the sleek and sexy new Karmann Ghias that just arrived in the VW showrooms.

They ogled several of the shiny Ghias at the dealership and fantasized about owning one — fantasized, because as a young struggling couple with their first child on the way there was no way they could afford one.

As they were leaving the dealership they noticed a woman selling wicker baskets on the very same corner. Although they couldn't afford a Ghia, they did buy a baby basket. This basket was my little corner of the world for the first few months of my life.

If there is any truth to the notion that children are affected by external forces in the womb, I may be proof. Today I am the owner of a Karmann Ghia parts and restoration business.

H. Scott Dempster

VIVA LA VOLKSWAGEN

In the late Fifties I lived in Brazil. Being a little girl, I had to go to school every day, like many other children, but there were not many, I believe, who were driven to school every morning by a chauffeur in a VW Bug.

The reason for this was that my Daddy was Walter Fischer, an executive for VW of Brazil. Oh, I was so mad because all the other little daughters and sons of the other car company directors came in these beautiful big and fancy cars and here was little old me in my Bug.

When I complained to my Daddy he would remind me how all those beautiful cars would overheat on the steep road that led from Santos (the beach) back to Sao Paolo every weekend. Those poor people would be stuck on the side of the road in the land of nowhere until their cars would cool down enough. Our little Volkswagen trucked by just like in a commercial.

It was big news when Brazil relocated its capital city. After years of planning to make Brasilia a modern, world-class place, the inauguration festivities were held April 20, 1960. Everyone wanted to be there. All the car companies in Brazil each sent two cars from the coast through the jungle on a dirt road, if you could call it that, to Brasilia to show off. My brother, Peter, was one of the drivers that my Daddy sent on this trip in the brand new VW buses. Headhunters had threatened this caravan and they had to drive through nothing but red mud. If my memory serves me right the only cars that made it to Brasilia and back were Jeeps and our VWs.

By the way — I just bought myself a 1959 VW Bug which I am having restored. I named it after my father, "Fritz", which was his middle name.

Steffi Smith

LABOR OF LOVE

During the 10 years we had our 1960 VW we had two children. One was born in '61 and the other in '63. Our son, the youngest, loved to crawl into the "well" behind the back seat and would usually fall asleep back there to the drone of the motor. I vividly remember how difficult it was to lift a four- or five-year-old out of there without waking him. My back still hurts just thinking about this but I'd gladly do it all again.

Dick Biedinger

THE MAGIC LEVER

Back in 1963 (I was 10), my parents owned a 1960, gray Volkswagen Beetle. I loved that car. My Dad loved it, too. I used to ride in the little compartment behind the back seat, before seat belts were mandatory. My Dad told me that area was designed just for me. I thought our Bug was the only one with that special compartment.

I was curious as to what you did with the lever between the front seats. Dad said that if there was a traffic jam, he could pull up on the lever, the car would raise and we would ride right over top of the other cars; thus avoiding the traffic jam. I remember being in stopped on a bridge over the Ohio River and begging him to use the lever. But he said "It could only be used once and we must save it for an emergency situation!" We never used the lever. I was much older before I realized the lever was actually an emergency brake.

My Dad is no longer with us but I still remember the magic he instilled in me as a child. The Volkswagen Beetle was definitely a source of good times for our family. I long for the days of riding around in that car with my Dad.

Lana Kaelin

BROTHERS IN CRIME

Around 1972 or '73 and my older brother was dating a girl who owned what is considered to an eight-year-old one of the coolest machines on the road: a 1970 blue Beetle.

One time when she came over to visit her heartthrob my younger brother and I discovered that her car was unlocked. So what do you suppose a red-blooded eight- and six-year-old did when faced with this discovery? Naturally, we climbed in, put it into neutral and away we went down the hill our house was atop. We coasted down the street and steered around the corner before coming to a stop. Fully aware of the magnitude of what we'd done, we ran like hell back to the house.

When the girlfriend came out after a couple of hours she discovered her car was gone. Of course she thought someone had stolen it. My little brother finally blew our cover when she was going to call the police. We didn't want to take any chances with being fingered by the fuzz.

Nevertheless, every time the girl came over and left it unlocked we went for a joyride.

Duane Hess

THEY CALL HIM MR. BUGG

Our late Dad, John W. Bugg, sold Volkswagen Beetles for several years at two dealerships in Louisville, Kentucky. We're sure there are many people who recall buying a Bug from Mr. Bugg. What a great story for them, although most people probably thought it was a joke initially. And what a great unintentional gimmick for Dad, as he did very well. He had many repeat customers.

We still have copies of the notes he used to send customers. They have a picture of him in one corner and a picture of a Beetle in the opposite corner. In between he would write personal messages, such as "Thank you for coming in." and "It was a pleasure to chat with you."

We have wonderful memories of Dad bringing home different demonstrators and the many different, brilliant colors of the Bugs, buses and fastbacks. We always had some sort of VW in our driveway.

Dad has been gone for more than 20 years but we always think of him when we see a VW.

Cindy (Bugg) Barnett and Kathy (Bugg) West

I want to thank you for coming in to discuss your transportation needs.

It was a real pleasure to "chat" with you, and if you have additional questions, please feel free to contact me.

John W. Bugg

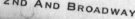

BROADWAY VOLKSWAGEN

2ND AND BROADWAY

DAD DRAGS THE KIDS AROUND WITH HIM

One time around 1970, my brother-in-law was the owner of a Bug. During his absence to attend National Guard training that summer, my sister, his wife, decided to drive it to visit our Grandmother. She lived about 10 miles from town. After the visit, my sister got into the Bug to go home but it would not start. She called someone to come and get her and left the car there to be picked up later.

When my brother-in-law returned home he, my father and I went to Grandma's to get the car. After several attempts to start it we decided to tow it into town to be fixed at a local garage. We used an 8- to 10-foot chain attached the front bumper of the Bug to the back of a utility pickup truck, the kind with the high toolboxes on either side of the bed. My father drove the truck, and my brother-in-law and I rode behind in the Bug. Being 12, I never missed an opportunity to ride in the VW.

My father, being a businessman and a farmer, was a hard worker with a high level of concentration. He was always busy so he never wasted any time. This day was no different. In his haste to get on with the business of the day, he forgot that we were behind him on a short chain, with little control of our car. Our speed soon reached 60 mph and we were scared to death. We tried to blow the born but it didn't work. My brother-in-law was constantly pumping the brakes to try to get Dad's attention. Nothing worked.

We soon came upon a slower-moving vehicle, and, much to our dismay, my very focused father pulled out into the other lane to pass. At that point I was almost too scared to move, but fear pumped the adrenaline through me and we began waving our arms out of the windows trying to get his attention. I stood up, with my head sticking out of the sunroof, and waved my arms wildly, losing my favorite cap in the process.

Just as the Bug got even with this car we were passing, my father must have seen us in his rear view mirror because he let off of the gas and fell back in behind the other vehicle. The person driving that other car must have thought we were crazy! It was like a scene from an old comedy movie. The last time that we looked at the speedometer, we were running at 70 mph.

I'll never forget the high-speed ride in the little Bug and getting that close to another vehicle with little or no brakes and no horn! We have laughed about this experience many times over the years but have never asked my father to tow me anywhere again.

James H. Graybeal

BICENTENNIAL BUS

In the 1970s when VWs were really common my father owned a '65 microbus camper. On the last day of school when I was only about six years old my mother and father would load it up with all the camping equipment and our clothes and meet us kids at the school to pick us up for our journey upstate to Roscoe, New York. We lived in Yonkers at the time so it was a long ride. We would play with the sink and open up all the little compartments in the back just to do something during the ride and the refrigerator always had juice in it for us kids in case we got thirsty.

When we got to the campsite we would help Mom and Dad set up the tents and run around in the fields to kill time but my favorite time was sleeping in the VW during thunderstorms. We were afraid of the lightning so Mom would throw us in the van for safety. My brother and I would sleep on the fold-down seat and my sister would sleep on the cot that stretched across the two front seats. It was such a cool van. Especially the pop top. My brother and I always used to fight over who got to open it.

I can remember in 1976 my father painted the bus red white and blue. We fit right in with the times, the bicentennial year.

We always had a VW. They are and always will be a part of my life.

Joe Cantinieri

TURNING TABLES ON DAD

I bought a 1967 Beetle when I was 15. I delivered pizzas to pay for it, and in the course of putting all the wear and tear on the little car it would break and cause me to have to ask my Dad for a tow home. He would always seize the opportunity to tell me to ditch the upholstered roller skate and buy a real car.

In 1975 my Dad bought a brand new Monte Carlo and one day it broke down. The dealer was a few miles away and I got the opportunity to tow him. There were all kinds of people watching as this puny little VW pulled away at that huge car. I remember them pointing and laughing. I took the long way there — past my buddy's house, where I slowed down a little. I may have forgotten that Dad had power steering on a few corners. Safely at the dealer he walked over and boldly hinted I may have driven too fast. I haven't let him forget it to this day.

My children think I bailed Papa out many times with the Bug — which I still have.

Steve Brown

TOUGH SCRAPE

My Mom had my bright orange 1974 VW Super Beetle repainted for me for $400. Delighted, I took it back to college with me.

As I was coming out of an alley on a side street, all these guys were standing on a side porch waving their arms and shouting. I thought, what in the world are these guys doing? I pulled out into the street and boom! I got sideswiped by a pizza delivery guy. He sideswiped the passenger side of the Volkswagen. I was devastated. The car wasn't dented but the paint had been totally swiped. I was very, very upset.

I worked with a girl who told me she knew a place that worked on VWs and painted them. So I called them. It was close to Thanksgiving break, and they said that yes, they could get it done. But it wouldn't be finished until Thanksgiving morning. I couldn't pick it up until then. I called my Mom and told her I wouldn't be able to come home until Thanksgiving Day. So I took the car in and they repainted it for me for $80, which to me, being a college student and only having a part-time job, was a lot of money. They had the exact color I needed and a friend of mine drove me over there to pick it up and he sat in his car and waited for me to make sure everything was OK.

I walked in the garage and this car looked absolutely beautiful. I was so excited! I thanked the guy over and over. He told me that when I pulled out of the garage to be very, very careful because it was a very narrow garage. So I said OK, and I hopped in. As I was pulling out — screeeecch — I scraped the entire side of the car. The *same* side was ruined all over again. I just sat there and put my hands on the steering wheel and cried. I looked over at my friend and he was laughing.

I sat there crying and thought, what can I do? I have to hide this side of the car from my Mom so she won't get upset that she wasted money painting the car.

I drove it home anyway, and parked so the good side was facing our front door. I told my older brother and sister about it and they thought it was hilarious. They promised not to tell her. I made it through the entire Thanksgiving break and Mom never saw the side that had been swiped.

I drove back to college thinking I'd get the car painted before Christmas. I'd save and earn the money somehow and get the car repainted so Mom would never know. Well, Monday morning I got a phone call. My Mom was outraged. "What did you do to the car? What in the world happened?" I asked her how she found out, if my brother and sister had told her. She said no, she had asked our neighbor what he thought of the car and what he thought of the paint job and he said, "Oh, it was great except for the scrape along the side."

What I'd hidden from my Mom was in plain sight of the neighbors!

There I was. Caught in my lie. My poor VW never got repainted. I drove it several years after that with the scrape along the side of it. It was kind of like its own little beauty mark. When I finally sold my VW, it was sold with its scar.

Jill Szturm

RIGHT PASSENGER, WRONG DOOR

In 1982, I found a '73 blue Beetle sedan for $1,500. I had learned that if you can find a good, honest mechanic, these Bugs will run forever. Unfortunately, I also learned that a good, honest mechanic is hard to find. But I kept that car about four years, finally giving it up for air conditioning and cruise control. But the thought of this little Bug always brings back a smile. Like the time my best friend and I went to a Christmas tree lot and picked out a six-foot tree. The boy at the lot said "What are you driving?" I pointed to the Bug. He shook his head and mumbled something about maybe being able to tie it on the back. Well, that wouldn't work because he couldn't find anything to tie it to. So, I decided to put it inside. It was a little hard to shift the gears, but the worst part was listening to my girlfriend complain all the way home because she had to sit in the back seat and I had "some tree that I didn't even know sitting up front". Then there were all the numerous times my Mom would start to get in on the driver's side because she always said she couldn't tell the front from the back!

I moved to Florida in this little car, taking almost everything I owned inside it. Mom and I used to take the car to the beach on the weekends. One time we decided to take a walk down the beach and as we were coming back we noticed a big crowd of people off in the distance. We wondered what could have happened. Did someone drown? Was there a shark attack? As we got a little closer, I saw a break in the crowd and through the people I saw my Bug, not only surrounded by spectators, but by the surf as well! The tide had come in and I was parked too close to the shoreline. I ran as fast as I could to the car and as I got there, the water was just starting over the running boards. I started it up, and with the help of about four very big guys, we were able to back it up into the dry sand. I got out and thanked everyone. They all got a good laugh out of the girl from up north that didn't know any better. In the meantime I started looking for my Mom, who I found standing at the back of the crowd saying "that silly girl, doesn't she know about the tide?" She waited for the crowd to clear out before she got in the car because she said she didn't want anyone to know she was with me!

But the funniest one was the day I took my Mom shopping in Orlando. We both were checking out at the store at the same time, but at different registers. She finished before me and went ahead outside. When I was done, I went outside expecting her to be waiting by the entrance. But she wasn't there, so I figured she must have gone ahead to the car. So I went out to the car and still no Mom. I looked back to the store entrance. No Mom. I looked around the parking lot. No Mom. By this time I was really starting to panic. So I got in the Bug and started driving around the parking lot, thinking maybe she had gotten turned around and was looking in the wrong aisle. Still, no Mom. Where could she be? Horrible thoughts were racing through my head. Had she been kidnaped? She's just a tiny little gray-haired retired woman, she'd be easy to overpower. Had she collapsed from the heat? Or her heart? I was beside myself with fear. And then it happened. I was driving down one of the aisles when I spotted her. She was sitting just as prim and proper as you please, minding her own business, in SOMEONE ELSE'S little light blue Bug! I pulled up beside her and Oh! If you could have seen the look on her face! She almost jumped out of her skin! I said "GET OUT OF THERE!" She got in my car and we laughed so hard I thought we'd die! She said she looked around the inside of the other car and didn't remember my car having so much trash in it! I wonder what would have happened if the other owner had gotten to her before I did!

Patti Rawlins

SQUATTER'S RIGHTS

In 1977, I was on a ride through New England with my grandmother to see the foliage in my red 1970 Beetle. We had toured all day through New Hampshire and were en route home to Boston well after dark.

We were on some dark unfamiliar road when my grandmother told me to hurry and find a gas station because she needed to "go" really bad. Well, there had been nothing on the road for what seemed like miles and I didn't expect another gas station anytime soon. She fidgeted and complained louder and louder. Up ahead I saw a clearing in the woods. I pulled in and through the darkness saw a huge wall that I figured was the back of a factory or some other business which had closed for the weekend.

Grandma got out, closed the door, lifted her dress, and rested her huge body against the running board.

Her sighs of relief were short lived.

A huge flood light engulfed us and a man's voice on a bullhorn barked "Put your hands where I can see them". My feisty grandmother let loose with a string of obscenities and was screaming to shut off the blankety-blank light.

Seconds later we were surrounded by men with guns. I had not known it but we had been on a private right-of-way and had pulled up to the rear wall of one of the state prisons.

When we were back on the road and the shock had worn off, we laughed all the way home.

Christopher Canary

BENNY

When my oldest son, Ted was about to enter college I began to look for a car he could use. Along came "Benny." He was a white '68 with an autostick transmission in great shape, but in need of a paint job. For some reason I was talked into painting it brown. Why, I'm not sure.

Anyway, Benny served us well for many years. He needed an overhaul once, which was done by a German mechanic whose expertise really revived it.

After my first son graduated my second son, Rob, drove Benny four more years to college even though he was almost sold once when the transmission went out. The fellow who said he would buy Benny never showed up so we had him repaired. Benny went back to college.

Another year went by before Rob loaned Benny to a girlfriend who ended up putting oil into the autostick transmission. Another repair was needed.

Then along came our youngest child, Megan, ready to go to college. Naturally, there was the perfect transportation for her — Benny. She drove him about two years or so. Benny was getting rusty.

But the final straw was probably one evening when Megan was driving this guy in a very fine suit to a friend's house. Before they hit the puddle she told her passenger to lift his feet. He didn't understand the holes in the floor like Megan did and therefore, got his pants all wet.

Time was running out on Benny. He was mechanically sound, but his body could no longer handle those Michigan winters around college campuses. The original $700 investment was sadly sold for $300 to another club member. What more could you ask?

After 11 years Benny deserved his own college degree. He

was our fourth child. My guess is that ugly, yet beautiful, brown Bug is still roaming some college campus and passengers are still picking up their feet when they go through puddles.

Bob Case

AUNT HAZEL

Many years ago I had an Aunt Hazel whom I loved very much. She was a very tiny lady with curly, white hair. When I purchased a white VW Beetle, it only seemed natural to name it after her. Like my aunt, the Bug was very unique. It seemed to have psychic powers. I recall a time riding with my sister when, out of the blue, she said, "If we were in a wreck, how would we get out of the car?" Within a matter of minutes, I turned a corner and hit another car. Another time, as we passed a building in the Bug, my sister said "that building looks like it's burning". That night it did.

One day I drove it into my driveway and parked it, kind of over to the side. I got up the next morning to find that my Beetle had mysteriously popped out of gear, rolled down a hill and smashed into a tree. At first I was angry because all the work I'd done on the car had been ruined. Later, I learned that my Aunt Hazel also died that day. The coincidence sent chills up my spine. It was a very strange, creepy happening.

Marianne Diehl Parker

FAMILY VALUES

Our 1973 Super Beetle witnessed many of the things that happened in our lives between 1977 and 1987. Its grand arrival into our lives was not planned out in advance. In fact, it was abrupt. Our "regular" car, which was only about two years old, needed a new engine. This was in the days before extended warranties. So there we were, packing for a very long summer trip (about 1,500 miles altogether) but without a functioning car; and without very much money either. A friend recommended his mechanic, Willie, who sold cars on the side. Whatever he had, it needed to be cheap. We knew that. Our friend advised us not to worry.

Willie showed us a Beetle that was faded with sizable dents in most of the fenders; a real survivor of city traffic. We weren't so sure about it. It certainly wasn't pretty. It ran very well, though. We liked Willie instantly, though, and trusted him. We took the car.

At home we spent a few hours cleaning the Beetle. We even used paste wax although we could not hide the dents. Our parents would not be very pleased about this acquisition. They were all big car people. We had been raised in the faith of the big car. Thus, little foreign cars were not "safe". At the very least we could make our new car appear neat and clean.

Then we took off on a summer trip that was about 700 miles on its first leg. No one seemed to even notice our new car and we didn't pursue the matter with anyone either. (His mother allowed that she'd always thought Beetles were cute.) The long ride seemed comfortable enough. Anyway, we were young.

A few months later there was an unexpected death in the family. The Beetle handled the trip just fine.

A year and a half later, we decided to move back to our home state 700 miles away. So we packed the Beetle with plants, luggage, and even a few small pieces of furniture. It was a good trip.

Over the next few years, we added a radio, had the dents repaired, and repainted the car. When our daughter arrived a few years after that, it was already 10 years old. At the age of three, her friends thought the Beetle was very exciting because it was so fast. Like other Beetles, ours usually seemed to be moving faster than it really was.

Our old Beetle seemed to represent some of our most closely held values, like simplicity and dependability. When the time came time to let it go, it kind of felt like we were losing someone very close.

Tom and Carolyn Louderback

TO A GOOD FAMILY

The first car I ever owned was a white 1968 Bug which I purchased for $800 when I was 17 in 1972. The seller was a woman who had begun to drive a new Mercedes. This beautiful, polished car had been kept up on blocks in a garage for two years until the nurse decided to let her Bug go "to a good family". I looked at my Dad and high school sweetheart and said "that's my car". My Dad wanted to negotiate prices and go for test drives, etc. I let him and my boyfriend do all that stuff but I knew I would own that car. When the transaction was completed I named the Bug "Adolph".

The day I brought him home my brother smashed in the front panel. My boyfriend fixed it before I even had a chance to kill my brother. A few weeks later I drove my sick baby sister through a blinding snowstorm down sidewalks and around construction. When I got stuck two burly guys simply picked up the front end and moved the car out of the snowdrift.

Adolph took me through nursing school, marriage to that same boyfriend and two babies. Finally, as finances improved and VW parts became scarce, we sold him in 1982.

In 1996 my husband took our 17-year-old daughter, Elizabeth, shopping for her first car. Elizabeth called me at work all excited. "Mom!" she squealed, "I bought a '66 Bug." When I told my fellow neonatal intensive care nurses about Elizabeth's "new" car every one of them had a VW story to tell. One of them had even owned five Bugs. Everybody was so excited for Elizabeth and confident that she had not just purchased a car but found a trustworthy friend.

Elizabeth's Bug had only had two previous owners. It came with a complete history written by the original owner. The history detailed travels across the Pacific and retirement to Florida. In Tallahassee, it was restored and auctioned off to raise funds for a local high school. The woman who sold it to Elizabeth had purchased it from the winner. Elizabeth got it for $1,200 — half the asking price. The owner knew this was all Elizabeth could afford and wanted the car to go "to a good family".

Elizabeth will leave for college soon. She will take her car with her and I am sure her car will take her through college, marriage and a couple of kids.

Recently my husband and I started to look for a new car for me. To say we experienced sticker shock would be an understatement. My husband refused to pay more for any car than the price of our first home. He also refused to buy any car that he can't work on. That's why he purchased a '72 Bug. When we were kids just going together I would talk to my husband and hand him his tools as he worked on cars. Yesterday, I was there for him when we repeated that scene as he worked on the transmission. This dear car is starting to take shape and to win a place in my heart.

We have also purchased another '72 to restore for our oldest daughter for a college graduation present. As I write this my husband and daughter are working on her '66. We have truly become a Bug family. Or have we always been a Bug family just now returning to our roots?

Sherry Zampino

CHAPTER SEVEN

WILD THINGS AND DOOR DINGS

Bug tales of animals and intrigue

THE BUGS AND THE BEES
AND A PONY IN A SQUEEZE

I left the seminary in 1959 and went to a (Lutheran) church in Rossville, Georgia. I believe that's where I first saw a Volkswagen and got interested in it. I bought a used one. Whenever it needed work I did it myself.

This was the only car in the family at the time; it was the main transportation for myself, my wife and our three kids. We once carried a whole davenport in it. But that wasn't the most unusual thing I ever hauled in it.

Around May of 1964 a man I knew had a pony. He let me have it for my kids. I figured we'd keep it in the back yard. But how could I get it home?

Well, I took up the back seat of the Bug and led the pony into it. It was a very docile thing, and had no problem getting into the car. It had no problem mistaking the floor for a field, either, so we got a deposit of "horse hockey" in no time.

Anyway, once I had the pony in back I headed home. But as soon as I pulled into traffic people starting staring. They could see me driving, and a pony. They couldn't believe it! I just figured that my 36-horsepower Bug was now 37 horsepower. I think we kept the car longer than the pony.

I transported something else unusual in one of my other VWs. You see, for many years I was a beekeeper. At any time I had six or eight colonies of bees in my backyard. Once while I was at a parish near Evansville, Indiana, my son Bob, who had bees, too, said he was going to move and he didn't want to keep his three colonies. So I headed to his house in Florence, Kentucky, in my Bug.

We put two of his hives in the back seat and one in the passenger seat. From my son's house to my house was about 200 miles. I went on down the road and eventually, around the time I got to Louisville, I needed to stop for gas. But I noticed that some of the bees had started getting out and were flying around in the car with me, landing on the seats and dashboard. They were on the windshield and the windows. Before I knew it the inside of my Bug was covered in bees!

This happened a long time ago, when there were attendants at service stations who pumped your gas for you. But when I pulled up to the pumps at a gas station all covered with bees and gas station attendant took one look and backed away. He wouldn't come near me!

I wasn't afraid because I knew how to handle bees but he was terrified. And he thought I was crazy. I just got out my credit card and slipped it through a slit in the window to him so I could get a fillup and be on my way. I never had any mechanical trouble on that trip. Just bee trouble.

Rev. John V. Roth (ret.)

BOSSY TAKES THE BUS

In the early 1970s my father had a '59 or so VW panel bus. We lived on a farm and we also had a milk cow. One bright, early morning Dad decided he wanted to move "Bossy" to a farm a mile or so away. His original plan was to tie Bossy to the bumper of the bus and slowly walk her to the destination. He threw some grain in a bucket and headed out to the pasture in the VW.

In the process of driving out to the cow, the bucket of grain slid to the side opposite of the bus's side doors. Bossy was used to being fed out of this particular bucket, so when Dad opened the doors and went to retrieve the grain from where it had slid, Bossy followed him right in. To get out of the way of the 1,200 pounds of advancing bovine, Dad opened the rear hatch and dove out. Meanwhile, Bossy made herself at home in the VW. Without a doubt, a 1,200-pound cow in a VW bus is a sight to see.

At this point Dad figured what the heck, she's in there, I might as well move her this way. After all, he did have to cross a major highway. This may actually be better.

To Dad's surprise, at the entrance to the highway sat the Missouri State Highway Patrol, checking license plates and such. Dad loved to trade cars so he rarely had proper plates on a vehicle and this one was no exception. He felt luck was with him though, since he knew the patrolman who stepped up to the window. Trying to avoid embarrassment and a long explanation, Dad was relieved that the patrolman couldn't see into the back of the van due to a curtain behind the front seats. Moments later his luck changed when Bossy lost her footing, making the van convulse under the strain. Startled, the patrolman asked Dad what in the world he had in there. Dad responded that he had, um, beef in there. The patrolman seemed satisfied with this and started to lecture Dad about the importance of proper licensing and such.

Before long, Bossy started to get uncomfortable. After all, her back was rubbing the roof of the van. She started shifting about trying to turn around so she would be facing forward. This made the poor bus look as if it were about to turn over. The patrolman jumped and exclaimed, "You've got something live in there!" He promptly ran to the rear of the van, looked in the small back window and nearly fell over at the sight of a rather large cow peering back at him.

After the patrolman's radio announcement of his find to the station, every patrolman in the area made their way to the site posthaste to see this wonder. Dad never got a ticket or anything. They seemed to have forgotten all about the license issue and apparently found there was no law on the books about taking your oversized cow for a ride in an undersized vehicle.

Word spread fast. Soon everyone knew that Ben Gulley got a cow in a VW. The officers never told anyone it was a VW bus, which only made the story more curious. Boy, did Dad have a hard time explaining that one away.

Benjamin Gulley Jr.

WOOL OVER OUR EYES

Back in 1982, I bought a '70 Bug from the original owner, a farmer who'd use it to take sheep to market one at a time in it. There was wool and sheep food in the back. The outside wasn't very impressive, either. Whenever the car needed touching up, the farmer would use whatever paint was available. That car had about 400 spots of different colored paint on it and was known as "Old Spot."

I spent all winter restoring it to its original condition and planned on a long road trip to Hilton Head, South Carolina in the spring. My girlfriend went with me and we drove with the top down all the way.

But about 30 miles from Hilton Head the car started acting really weird. I pulled off the road where I saw a light. I figured there might be a gas station there. I was preoccupied with looking in the engine compartment, where there were burned wires. At first I didn't look up. But when I did, I saw about a million moths about the size of silver dollars. They were as thick as I could see and were drawn to the candle my girlfriend had lit to see. Or maybe they were still looking for the farmer's wool.

I got my tool kit and electrical tape and worked on the car. All the while moths were crawling down our backs and swarming around us. My girlfriend started to scream. It was like a bad 1950's science fiction movie.

Finally I got it started and we went on to Hilton Head and the condo where we were going to stay. As I unloaded, every time I closed a door or opened the glove box of the car moths would come out. They were in the fender wells and in the trunk, too. It seemed like they would even come out of our suitcases. We hadn't left them behind. They came with us.

When it was time for us to go home we were on the road in

Knoxville, Tennessee when the car started acting up again and eventually broke down. We walked to an exit where we found three guys in a garage, drinking. They got in their pickup truck, tied a rope around the axle of my Bug and towed it back to their garage. They said my alternator was bad and that it would cost me $350. But my car had a generator, not an alternator. They didn't know anything. But they did try to get my girlfriend to drink their moonshine.

I fixed the wires with new tape and got ready to go again. They said I owed them $25 for the tow and $15 for the electricity from their garage that I used to see when I fixed the car myself. It was a disaster. And my girlfriend was drunk.

Eventually we made it home. My girlfriend slept the whole way. The next day I went out to check my car and when I opened the hood a giant moth flew out. It had ridden back with us as a souvenir of this terrible trip.

Mark C. Fisk

AS SNUG AS A GERBIL IN A BUG

My mother bought a 1966 Volkswagen Beetle sedan. It was black with a red basket weave interior and was purchased new in '66 for the reasonable price of around $1,600. My mother bought this car to be the economical and reliable car that Volkswagen meant it to be. It was so basic it didn't even have a radio.

My family was a close-knit group. At Christmas, we would alternate the family gathering between our house and my aunt's house. Winter in Chicago can be frigid and our little Beetle's heater was no match for the below-freezing temperatures on this particular Christmas Eve. It was my aunt's turn to host the festivities.

The day before, my Mom had picked up my grandparents and brought them back to our house. After the presents were wrapped and loaded into the Bug my mom, grandparents and I (dressed in our Sunday best and winter coats) piled into that little car, scraped the frost from the INSIDE of the windshield, and headed off. After dinner, the presents were opened and much to my surprise, my cousin had given me a gerbil. It came with a book on how to care for it, a supply of food and a small cardboard box with some holes punched in it to take my new pet home. At eight years old, I was excited to have the responsibility of caring for this wonderful new pet.

At the end of the evening, Mom went out to warm up the Beetle. We debated on whether or not to leave the gerbil at my aunt's house until the weather warmed up, but we decided to wrap his cardboard box with a small blanket and head for home. My grandmother, in her fur coat, sat in the back with my new pet and me. My grandfather, in his wool overcoat, rode shotgun in the front with my mother driving. With the presents, that car was packed like a can of sardines!

Everyone was tired and my grandmother and I both fell asleep during the ride home. Mom woke us upon our arrival and the No. 1 priority was to get that gerbil in the house before he froze. When I got in the house I opened the box and my new pet was gone! Mom and Grandad retraced our steps through the snow with a flashlight but to no avail. They looked under the seats in the Beetle and even up under the dash. Still no luck.

My grandmother was inside trying to console me, but I was hysterical. The situation looked hopeless but my grandfather took one more look under the seat with the flashlight and lo and behold, my new Christmas present popped his head out of the rear seat heater vent. He was no dummy. He knew just where to go to stay warm. With a little coaxing, Grandad was able to retrieve him from his cozy hiding place and bring him inside. We were all thankful the gerbil didn't get trapped in the heater channel because there would have been an unpleasant reminder of him circulating throughout the car every time we turned the heater on.

Kirk and Pam Schulz

KING OF THE BEASTS FINDS A ROLLING THRONE

I was on a road trip with my boyfriend near Sandusky, Ohio. The year was 1970 and we were driving my beige '66 Bug. Looking for something to do on a sleepy Sunday, we came across a billboard advertising a drive-through African safari. The sign featured lions and other wild beasts walking freely around a line of cars in an open field. This appeared to be the perfect thing to satisfy our craving for adventure.

We followed the directions to the safari and to our surprise the advertisement wasn't exaggerating. After paying a fee, you listened to an orientation, then actually drove on a paved path into some heavily fenced acreage where you could observe the animals up close from the relative safety of your car. We were assured that the animals were used to cars passing through, and almost never bothered them, but naturally the facility couldn't be responsible in the unlikely event that damage was caused. This was better than we had ever expected.

About half way through, we came to a pack of lions. I was amazed how close they were and began taking pictures. Suddenly we were startled by a violent jolt from the back of the Bug as if we were hit by another car. To our horror, we turned to witness a full-grown male lion with a huge mane climbing the back of my Bug. He came to rest across the rounded top of the Beetle crushing it in like an aluminum can in the shape of his massive belly. Hanging over the flat windshield were his two paws the size of dinner plates. Out the back window we observed his powerful swishing tail. Scared? Oh yeah, we were scared. At any minute we were sure the roof was going to come in even further or he was going to put one of those paws through the windshield and retrieve the trembling human snacks inside.

After what seemed like an eternity, the lion got bored with

observing his domain from this rounded perch and dismounted across the front, crushing the hood as he went. Needless to say we didn't get out to take pictures as this happened but we at least had proof for our friends at home. After reaching the safety of the parking lot outside we exited the Bug to find it covered with dents and muddy paw prints. Fortunately, most of the dents were able to be popped out, but for years I loved to show off the remaining battle scars on the roof and hood. I never dreamed of having them fixed completely, they were a real conversation piece and gave the car personality.

Eventually I sold the Bug to my brother, who proudly showed off the dents for another five years. My brother and I both got a lot of mileage out of that old Bug, but even more out of retelling its ordeal.

My boyfriend and I set out for adventure that day. We got more than our money's worth.

Chris Freel

IT MAY LOOK LIKE BUTTER — BUT IT'S (S)NOT

It seems like EVERYONE over the age of 35 had a Beetle at some time or another! I'm no exception. I've had several over the years. I'm currently driving a white 1970 one. I don't know of any other car that gets as much reaction from people, good or bad, young or old.

Likewise, I don't know of any other car that's gotten as much attention from livestock as my very first Bug, a '64 that I paid $600 for in 1975.

I am an artist by profession, and many years ago I used to love visiting my boyfriend's family farm on weekends. There was always interesting material to draw. One time I drove it over there, parked in the pasture, and hauled my sketchbook and stool into an abandoned house on the property and went to work.

After some time passed I kept hearing a buzzing sound. Eventually the noise got pretty annoying and, in looking around to find out what it was, I discovered I'd set my stool on top of some boards that had bumblebees nesting underneath. They were getting a little ticked off and started coming out of their nest so I grabbed my stuff to make a quick exit.

But there was Snowflake, the big Charolais bull in the doorway! I had to get to the Bug fast so I took off out the window. When I got to the car I just had to laugh. While I had been sketching the herd of cows became really curious about that big piece of metal in their pasture. I didn't know this, but to "investigate" something, cows will LICK IT.

There was my Bug, surrounded by a half-dozen cows slurping and slobbering all over it. Roof, doors, lights, windows, mirrors — every inch of that car was covered in cow slobber and snot. I had to wait them out.

Driving back to the main house, I could hardly see through

all that slime. The only thing anyone said was that I was lucky Snowflake didn't try to romance my car and crush the roof in!

Margaret Schryver

DOGGONE BUG

In March of 1969, my husband Larry and I had just been married for a year. Together with our six-month-old Dachshund "Fritz" we were moving cross country to San Diego for Larry's new job and our new life.

We had carefully packed our belongings into our new '69 Beetle. The trunk was full and the back seat was packed to the top of the high-back front seats. You couldn't get another thing in that car. On top of the pile was a flat area where Fritz would lay on his favorite silk quilt positioned perfectly to view the road ahead.

With Dallas some miles ahead in the middle of the night, Fritz began to get fidgety. Larry reached back and gave him a peppermint candy to keep him busy. Weary from the road, we were unaware that Fritz had lost hold of his candy, allowing it to tumble down a tight crevice all the way to the rear floorboard. Being long, skinny and determined, he rooted his way down a narrow passage between boxes toward the scent of the candy. Some time had passed before we heard his muffled cries and turned to find only the tips of his back paws and tail visible. We tried to pull him up as we drove but it was useless, he was stuck.

Before all the blood rushed to Fritz's little head we pulled over on one of the busiest stretches of four-lane interstate in Dallas. Even with the car stopped we were unable to dislodge Fritz. Our only choice was to start unloading. With cars breezing by, we began removing boxes until we exposed enough of Fritz for Larry to get a grip on his back legs. With a gentle pull, Fritz emerged with the peppermint in his mouth and a triumphant look on his face.

I've never seen Larry so mad. Here we sat with our earthly belongings piled along the highway in the middle of the Texas night all because Fritz had to have his candy. It seemed like it took forever to reload the Bug but we eventually did and made it to our destination.

We kept the Bug for only a few more years but Fritz lasted another 16.

Today, whenever I see a VW Beetle I think of old Fritz on that March night alongside the road. It always brings a smile.

Brenda Simpson

IN YOUR FACE

Back in the winter of 1979, I was a senior in high school and I got "the Bug". The car was in really bad shape. It was kept in an old chicken coop and was very dirty. When I found the owner, I was shocked that he only wanted $50 for it. I figured I couldn't go wrong at that price.

I had the car towed home and stripped it down to the bare bones. I wanted to rebuild it from scratch. I bought another Beetle with front end damage and transferred parts to the other one.

Finally, the car was almost finished. I was waiting for a gasket to come so I could install the windshield and the bumpers needed some welding done on them. I didn't have a welder; but I had a friend who did. He lived only three miles up the road. One day, he offered to do the welding I needed to have done.

I still didn't have the windshield in, but, I thought "It's a beautiful day and it's only three miles. What could happen?"

I started up the winding back road to his house. It was great. The sun was shining down on me and the wind blowing through my hair. The car was purring and handling great.

Suddenly, there it was. I had just gone over a hump in the road and there was the fattest robin I had ever seen. It was right in the middle of my lane.

I must have surprised it as much as it surprised me. It started to fly, but not fast enough. It came right through the space where the windshield should be and hit me square in the face.

Hurt? I couldn't believe it. I was on the brakes hard, holding the wheel with one hand and my face with the other. My glasses were on the floor. I finally got stopped and found my glasses.

I looked back and saw the robin panting on the back seat. It was as shocked as I was. It flew off and I drove on to my friend's house. He couldn't stop laughing when I told him what happened.

That was almost 19 years ago and I still have the car.

Dave Shirk

IT'S A CIRCUS OUT THERE

During the Seventies I lived and worked in suburban Pittsburgh and usually listened to the evening news on my car radio while commuting. One evening the "story on the lighter side" addressed a police call to investigate a report that "An elephant is sitting on my car." On investigation, the police confirmed that the report was not a hoax or a joke, but in fact, was true!

The circumstances were that the circus had just come to town. It arrived by railroad, and to promote its appearance a parade was conducted between the railroad yard and the Civic Arena where the performances were given. One of the acts included an elephant that, on cue, would "sit" on an orange pedestal. When this particular elephant approached an orange VW Bug that was parked along the parade route — you guessed it — it broke ranks and immediately set down on the Bug's nose and crushed it. The horrified owner called the police to document the incident explaining "How else would you ever get your insurance company to believe a story like this?"

William G. Tope

CHAPTER EIGHT

NOW PLAYING

Bug tales of the playful and bizarre

AN IDLING BUG IS THE DEVIL'S WORKSHOP

My story starts out on Christmas Eve, 1969. My friend, Dave, and I went to pick up our girlfriends from midnight Mass. While we were waiting outside we enjoyed the benefits of malt and hops.

We looked around in the cold moonlight. We admired the steeple. We listened to the radio. We wondered how long midnight Masses could last.

It was boring and we were just two wiseguys. Then, almost simultaneously, we noticed the double-wide doorways on both sides of an enclosed hall that connected the rectory and church. The hallway bisected the parking lot.

A wide opening. A small car.

Hmm.

I looked at Dave. Dave looked at me.

We reached the same conclusion. We've gotta try to get there from here. We've gotta see if the Bug would fit.

I got behind the wheel. It's impossible to be stealthy in a 1960 Beetle so I had to be quick. I easily made it through the first doorway.

Did we fit? Yes.

Did we come out the other side? Well, no.

When I tried to emerge through the second set of doors, I couldn't get around two cars parked at an angle on the other side. My only option was to back through the way I came.

As I threw the Bug into reverse I heard and felt something awful. The rear and front bumper were scraping on the side of the doors.

I pulled forward and backward a couple of times, trying to get out. No luck. I'd never realized until then how loud a VW engine is in an enclosed space. Especially at church. Especially at midnight.

There was no time to panic. I jumped out, Dave and I picked up the rear of the car and aligned it with the opening. Where our brains failed our muscles didn't. I jumped back behind the wheel to complete my retreat. Hallelujah!

Our relief at solving the problem was short-lived, however. When our girlfriends finally came out of church they asked if we knew what all the noise had been about.

I looked at Dave. Dave looked at me.

We appeared to be the only suspects.

Maybe it was the malt and hops, but we crumbled under the interrogation and confessed. The girls weren't surprised. Or terribly amused. Especially when they informed us our rumbling Bug was only 20 feet away from the pine-bedecked pews. We knew it had been loud but never dreamed it had been THAT loud. The girls said the noise had nearly drowned out the hymns and stopped the Mass.

It was a Christmas miracle that the authorities hadn't been called. I surely hope St. Peter has a poor memory when my time comes.

Michael C. Patton

YOU CAN ALWAYS COUNT ON
THE GUYS AT WORK

A guy I worked with got a brand new '72 Super Beetle.
Shortly after he got it, I'd see the guys from his department sneak
out every morning with a five-gallon gas can. I had no idea what
was going on so one morning I followed them out to the parking
lot. After witnessing what was happening, they told me they had
been draining small amounts of gas out of the Super Beetle and
hiding it just to see if their coworker would notice.

At the time, I drove a Karmann Ghia. One day the new Super
Beetle owner pulled me aside and asked me, "What kind of gas
mileage do you get?" I told him I got about 26 miles per gallon
in the city. He looked at me, shook his head, and said "I'm down
to eight miles per gallon." He took it back to the dealership and
told them what he was experiencing. They checked out the whole
car and couldn't find anything wrong so they suggested
monitoring the gas mileage again for several weeks. After all, it
was a new car and may just need breaking in.

He continued driving the car and the symptoms mysteriously
disappeared. Meanwhile, the dirty rascals back in his
department decided they couldn't just let this die. They got out
the trusty five-gallon can once again, only this time they started
adding gas. Some time later, the guy proudly came up to me and
said "You say you're only getting 26 miles per gallon? I'm
getting 43." He wasn't complaining now.

Those rascals did that to the poor guy for about three
months. Finally some time after they quit messing with him, he
confided in me that he was sure glad that car calmed down. It
almost drove him nuts. The car went from 8 to 43 miles per
gallon before it finally settled down to around 27. He never
caught on.

Mel and Rosalie Butler

TOP SECRET NAVAL ENGINE OPERATION

I went into the Navy in 1968, right out of high school. Soon after, I was stationed at Great Lakes Naval Base in Waukegan, Wisconsin, where I was being trained as a diesel engine technician. Little did I know but that meant they were going to put us on little boats in Vietnam to work on diesel engines.

My younger brother back in Ohio had a VW with a tired engine. To occupy our free time a fellow trainee named Peter and I decided we'd build the best high-performance VW engine ever made and deliver it to my brother on a weekend off. Extra incentive for Peter came from my wife-to-be, Ann, who promised to introduce him to her best friend upon making the eventual Ohio delivery. There were only two problems: We didn't have a spare VW engine to work with and any such personal projects are forbidden on the base.

Fully aware of our obstacles, Peter and I traveled to a junk yard in Milwaukee and bought an intact VW engine that had come out of a wrecked 1965 Bug. Nothing special, just a standard, well-used VW engine. Problem number one was solved but problem number two proved to be much more of a challenge. The engine was greasy and nasty from neglect so we wrapped it in plastic and maneuvered it into the folded-down back seat of Peter's VW Beetle. Our next step was to somehow sneak the engine back onto base and into our barracks, where we could occasionally work on it without tipping off the petty officers and bigwigs.

We managed to get back on base but decided we would keep our purchase in Peter's Bug until we knew the coast was clear. Finally one night around midnight we made our move. The cubicles in our barracks had big metal lockers to store our belongings. We had the good fortune of having access to a couple unclaimed lockers. We knew as long as we had a lock on the container nobody would pay much attention to it so we smuggled the engine in and put it in the nearest empty locker, placing a nice heavy lock on it.

Having successfully moved the engine, our next job was to start taking it apart. We actually borrowed — we didn't steal, we borrowed — tools from the base, since during the day we were working in the engine facility and had access to any tool you could ever imagine. Before we would leave for the day, we'd fill our pockets with tools and come out with all we needed for that night's work. We grabbed a bite to eat and long about 7 p.m. we'd pull this nasty engine out, put it up on a study table and start taking it apart.

At least by having the engine broken down we were able to determine what parts were needed. We got off at about 3 p.m. and if we didn't have to stand duty, we'd bust out and buy whatever we needed during the day. A problem we still had to face was the hundreds of greasy parts we had stored on shelves and in lockers all over the barracks. The key to this operation hinged on finding some way to clean these pieces. We knew we couldn't use gasoline or any solvents in the barracks or we could get into serious trouble and leaving the base each day with greasy parts didn't seem practical.

Finally we devised a most ingenious plan. Each night when we'd go in to take a shower would each bring two or three pieces along with cleanser we'd borrow from the supply area. We'd go in and sit our tails on the floor and scrub these pieces under a hot shower. It was kind of relaxing other than the fact that you were sitting there naked scrubbing engine parts. It worked surprisingly well, especially on the aluminum parts. It took us almost three weeks to get the pieces clean. As we'd bring them back, we'd put them into what we came to know as our "clean parts locker" on a different side of the barracks. It was quite a system.

We wanted to make this a high performance engine, so we

needed special parts. On weekends we'd make the trip to
Chicago to the headquarters of one of the most famous auto
parts retailers in the world, The Warshawsky Company (J.C.
Whitney). What an experience! You'd walk in and it would
seem like there were hundreds of people there. You would take
a number like you were in a bakery, grab a clipboard and list the
parts you wanted. Then you'd hand in your clipboard and in five
minutes, even most obscure and hard-to-find parts came rolling
down a conveyer. It was unbelievable! In one trip we could get
everything we needed and have time stop by Peter's Mom's
house in South Chicago to sample one of her "old country"
recipes. Who could ask for better?

After about two months, we had the project finished. By
now it was December and we were ready to make the long-
planned weekend trip to Ohio to deliver the motor. We got off
early that Friday and prepared Peter's Bug for the trip.
Retrieving the completed engine from its hiding place, we got
on either side of it and began carrying it toward his Bug.
Making our way down some stairs, we came face to face with a
lieutenant coming up. Upon taking notice of our strange cargo,
he bellowed, "Where in the hell are you guys going and what in
the hell is that?" Without stopping, I nervously responded,
"Well, sir, we have to get this engine out to that VW and deliver
it. It's very important." Puzzled by my answer, he asked "Well,
where did it come from?" Still making our way toward the door
I said "Sir, this engine is heavy, we've got to get moving or
were going to drop it." He followed us all the way to the car
barking questions as he went.

Reaching the VW, Peter and I went through the now-
familiar routine of manhandling the engine into the folded rear
seat area. The lieutenant never stopped talking but at this point
hadn't gotten our names. Once the contraband was loaded, I
whispered to Peter "Start this SOB up." I jumped into the
passenger seat, Peter popped the clutch and we were gone.

On the way to Ohio, it started snowing heavily. We weren't too concerned knowing the traction that VWs got with the engine in the rear. Hell, here we were with two engines in the rear. We decided to keep on going.

Up ahead we saw a jack-knifed truck. We were in the center lane. I'm not sure what happened next but suddenly we found ourselves sliding sideways straight down the highway at about 45 mph toward the truck.

With nerves of steel, Peter calmly spun that VW completely around and came right back into the center lane like a toy slot car. Missing the truck, we kept on going but at a much slower pace. The normal six-hour drive took almost 10 hours but we made it alive.

The trip was not in vain. My brother was thrilled with his new engine. He installed it in his car and quickly gained the reputation of having the fastest VW around. Peter's payoff came when he was finally introduced to Ann's best friend Jean. They fell very much in love, and are happily married to this day.

Nothing ventured, nothing gained.

Stephen F. Overbeck

PASSING INSPECTION

I had a 1960 Volkswagen Beetle whose horn would not beep when the car was idling. At that time, our town had an ordinance that said cars had to pass an inspection every six months.

Once, I took time during my lunch hour, with three co-workers accompanying me, to run my VW through the inspection lane. There was quite a long line of cars waiting, which meant that mine was idling for a considerable length of time. Over and over again we heard the drill: Lights! Wipers! Horn!

When it finally became my turn, I switched on the lights. "OK," the attendant checked off on his list. I turned on the wipers. "OK."

Then he told me to blow the horn. Right on cue, one of my compatriots in the rear seat yelled "Beep" and the attendant just kept going. "Horn. OK..."

I received a windshield decal which meant my VW was approved for another six months!

Dick Biedinger

HOOKED ON MY BUG

One summer morning in 1974 I was leaving the house for work in my dark blue '69 Volkswagen Beetle. It was the first car I ever owned and I thought I was hot stuff driving it down the road.

This particular morning I was running behind schedule. Even the chance of being late for work always made me nervous.

I was a teller at a savings and loan. All of my coworkers and I had to take turns stopping at the post office to get the office mail before we opened for business. On this morning, it was my turn. Hurriedly, I pulled my VW up in front of the post office, which was on a one-way street with the post office on the right side. I rushed in and got the mail, came back out and hopped in the car. I dumped the mail on the passenger seat. I grabbed my purse and began looking for my car keys. I searched and searched. This was so strange. They had to be right there! Another minute passed and for some reason, I just happened to look up. I noticed that the van parked in front of me was beginning to back up. "Surely he won't hit me," I thought.

I assured myself that it was nothing to worry about. Besides, I had other worries right now, namely, my keys. I resumed my search. Disgusted that I was having no luck, I glanced up at the van again. It was getting closer and closer to my car. I thought to myself, "Man, he's going to hit me! He doesn't even know I'm here!" I wanted to blow my horn to let him know that I was behind him, but I couldn't. Unfortunately, VW horns don't blow unless the keys are in the ignition.

Out of frustration I turned my purse upside down and held it by two corners. I dumped everything out of it but it was too late. The van's bumper went over the top of my bumper and off

the driver went. He may have thought he was pulling out alone but he wasn't. I was right there with him.

The driver was dragging me down the street unaware I was even there. I couldn't blow my horn. I had no keys. The only thing I could do was open the car door, hang out, wave my arms frantically and yell.

Finally — finally! — after the van took my Bug three blocks or so, the driver saw the commotion in his left side mirror. While in a state of shock and disbelief I could see the driver in his side mirror, kind of laughing. This upset me even more because I didn't think it was a bit funny at all. First, I started the morning out by already being late for work. Now, because if this, I was extremely late for work, a block past where I want to be on a one-way street, and I was hooked onto someone else's van and couldn't get off. Believe me. It was not EVEN funny.

It didn't take long before the driver noticed that I was not laughing and he calmly proceeded to unhook our vehicles.

I finally walked into the savings and loan and approached my boss. He had always been a really cool, understanding guy, so I didn't hesitate to explain to him that the reason I was late for work was due to a strange incident that happened to me when I was stopped at the post office to get HIS office mail. I tried to make it sound as if it was his fault. After all, I was doing it for him, right?

Patiently, he asked what happened. Nicely, I explained that I was dragged down Monmouth Street three blocks by a van.

He just looked at me and said, "Sure you did, Mary Ann." Then he continued, "I have heard some far-fetched 'late' stories but yours beats them all!" To this day, he still does not believe I was telling the truth. Mr. Egan, if you are reading this, I WAS telling the truth. Really, I was.

Mary Ann Geiman Stulz

SEATLESS IN ARMONK

Having started work for IBM Corp. in New York City in 1961, I was delighted to be promoted seven years later to the corporate headquarters in rural Westchester County, New York, specifically the village of Armonk, 35 miles north. We had relocated to our new home in Yorktown Heights and I purchased a new, white '68 VW.

My wife had, over an extended period, of time "suggested" that I acquire one or more new business suits to both replace those which had served well in the past. Plus, I was at corporate headquarters where only "rebels" occasionally would appear in the hallway without their suit coats!

Nonetheless, I was not and never would be a clothes horse. Getting me to a haberdashery was not an easy task. Peer pressure, along with spousal suggestions and the dripping water torture, prevailed. I set a date with three other new friends to go to Barney's in New York — the seven-story Mecca of men's clothing stores.

I had finished my day's tasks, cleared my desk of all documents, locked my desk drawers, put the trash container in the hallway and locked my office door. I was off to the parking lot and my meeting with my friends for the shopping trip.

Approaching my Bug, I noticed the passenger side door was partly open and rebuked myself for such carelessness. Coming closer and opening the driver's side door, I discovered a wide expanse of emptiness where the two front seats had been. I must have stood there a full minute, filled with awe at the rather large void created by the missing seats, given the diminutive overall size of the Bug in total.

This must be a joke. I was sure that somewhere, probably within sight, there would be an explanation or solution. The seats would magically appear or a friend would drive up with

them and I would be the butt of some good-natured fun. No one
— or seats — reappeared. A few coworkers stopped, looked,
smiled and went on their ways.

Regardless of the situation, I decided to get in and be on my
way. I had an appointment at Barney's!

I imagine most people in this world have never tried to start
a standard transmission automobile while sitting on the floor
without seats. For the uninitiated, it IS possible! Life does
however, become much more difficult once the engine is started
and you wish to see over the dashboard. All that's required is a
navigator who can see the road. Being someone who had
recently been promoted to corporate headquarters, I realized this
was a difficult, if not impossible situation.

Back in my office, I telephoned my wife, corporate security,
and the local police, in that order. It's a wonder that the second
and third calls ever were completed. My wife Kathleen took the
news that the seats had been removed/stolen with considerable
calm. I later learned that she considered my tale a clever method
for deviating from the Barney's excursion. She agreed to notify
my friends and offered up the questions "What are you going to
do?" and "How are you going to get home?"

I replied that I was going to go downstairs to the computer
center and see if I could "borrow" enough boxes of computer
paper (solid, heavy, etc.) which would serve as a platform on
which I might sit. While not having long considered this idea, it
seemed like a good first try. Surely, the world's largest computer
maker would be able to lend a needy employee a box or two of
paper.

Out in the parking lot with a dolly and a full set of boxes, I
found that two boxes set side by side would make a somewhat
stable bench substitute for the absent bucket seats with head
rests. By placing the boxes on top of the seat rails I had a trough
I could sit in yet still see over the dashboard. Once I returned
the unnecessary boxes and secured the seat belt, I was on my

way, albeit hunched over.

The trip home was completed successfully once I discovered and mastered the technique of left and right turns. Right turns were easy once contact with the driver's door was made. However, swift lefts were much more interesting as there was nothing but the seat belt and the floor-mounted gear shift to prevent one from sliding toward the passenger side. An open window and left elbow outside on the door developed into an effective but somewhat dangerous technique. A third arm and hand would have raised the safety element.

Naturally, there was considerable awe upon arriving home. My wife discovered that I really was missing the front seats. Several friends visited that evening to view the unlikely sight. The next day, my insurance agent accepted my report in a more routine manner than was anticipated. He suggested I get replacement seats from the VW dealer. This seemed practical and a good suggestion. The dealer responded that he didn't have seats or even the components and suggested either a special order or a junk dealer as possible solutions.

The police informed me that a group of local "entrepreneurs" had realized that the new VW bucket seats with head rests were both easily removed and highly prized by "hippies". It seemed they would fit easily and nicely into their popular VW vans which served as mobile homes for Sixties youth. I was informed that I was the latest victim of a local but widespread epidemic of parking lot VW seat thefts.

This explained the replacement "shortage" at the dealer and the junkyard's zero inventory.

Several weeks later and with significantly improved cornering techniques, I received from the dealer two seats assembled from assorted components for the then-considerable price of $350.

Although my new seats were easily installed, the replacement seat rails never exactly matched the rails on the floor such that quick acceleration or stopping caused an occupied seat to slide forward or backward several inches before catching and holding.

While my family was aware of this, any new passenger had to be warned, hopefully in advance about the "loose" seat, which served as an ongoing reminder of my carelessness. I cannot remember ever failing to lock my '68 VW once the replacement seats were installed.

We lock our present cars 99.9% of the time and I haven't had a seat stolen since!

Douglas E. Hall

LARD HAVE MERCY!

In the Seventies I was working with a man who raised pigs on the side. Besides his day job he had a farm and about 100 pigs. He never slept, this guy.

Once a year he'd sell some of these pigs on foot. They cost only 52 cents a pound. I was always trying to save a buck to feed my family and that seemed like a good deal, so I asked him to set me up with one pig. He said here's what we do: we slaughter and process the pig, and then you come and pick up the meat. So there I went, with my little white Bug.

He had all the meat wrapped up nicely for freezing purposes. Then he handed me a two large buckets. It was lard. I wasn't sure what I was going to do with it but I figured it was mine so I took it. It looked solid to me. I had no idea it was liquid; I paid no attention. It was white, just like a candle. I loaded everything in the back seat of my VW and drove home.

On the way home I began smelling something but I didn't realize what it was. I started to unload the neatly wrapped bundles and made a horrible discovery. My buckets of lard were empty! The inside of my car was coated with the stuff.

I was desperate. My whole family laughed at me while I tried to scoop up all that lard. It took days to get most of it out. Eventually, the winter set in and the remainder started to get more solid. It took me several more months to clean all of it out.

I kept that Bug for 10 years and it never once failed to get me to work. It never really lost that "beautiful" smell, but then again it never rusted.

George Thiemann

UNDESIGNATED DRIVER

In the summer of 1976 I was 18 years old. I had just gotten my first car a month before. It was a '69 light blue little Volkswagen Bug.

One really hot day, a friend and I decided to go lay out in the sun in a secluded area of a nearby park. Before leaving the last thing my mother said to me was "Don't be late for dinner. No excuses".

While laying out in the sun in our little bikinis we heard a car door slam. We thought somebody had pulled in behind our car or something so we grabbed our towels and started to run toward it. We discovered that there was no other car but someone was sitting on the passenger side of mine.

Very tentatively we walked over to the car since we had no clue who it was. We got to the driver's side window and saw it was an older lady wearing a big sun hat. My friend and I looked at each other and then I leaned down and said, "Excuse me, ma'am. Can I help you with something?"

No answer. I thought, oh my God what do I do now? Then, all of the sudden, the lady flung herself back in the seat and threw her arms back. My girlfriend thought she had a gun in her hand so she hit the dirt. Again I tried to communicate with the lady but she still wouldn't respond. Meanwhile, my friend kept the situation calm by yelling, "She's got a gun! She's got a gun!"

Just then a Cadillac pulled up. The woman inside it asked "Have you seen a lady with a big sun hat?" I said "Yeah! She's in my car, does she belong to you? The woman said no but that she had witnessed the sunhat lady sitting in the middle of the road and thought she needed help. She turned around and came back to find her but she was gone.

Then the three of us tried to talk to the sunhat lady but she still wouldn't say a word. The whole time we were still wearing only our bathing suits because our clothes were in the car. We accepted the offer of the woman with the Cadillac to drive us to the nearest gas station to call the police. We made the call and patiently waited (still in our bathing suits) at the gas station for the police to come and take us back.

By the time we got back, my little Bug was SURROUNDED by five police cars and one ambulance. We were just dying. We had no clue what was going on. One of the police finally said they had been looking for this lady for a couple of days. She apparently had a pass from a local mental hospital for the weekend and hadn't returned.

She was strong and it took them a long time to get her out of my Bug. For at least an hour she fought them destroying my dash, shift knob and seat in the process. Then, suddenly it was over, all the police cars left and we were just standing there. Everybody was gone. My friend and I got back into the car and drove home without talking too much. I'm certain we were both thinking the same thing, "What the hell just happened here and how will we explain it?"

By the time I got home I was a half hour late for dinner. I told my mother the story while remembering the warning she gave me before we left. She just shook her head and gave me with one of those "Is that the best you can do" kind of looks that only mothers can give. It took a number of years but at least now I think she finally believes me.

Joy

HOOD ORNAMENT

While attending college in the mid-70s in upstate New York, I owned a 1971 VW Bug, which was a great car to have during the cold winter months because of the good starting capability and excellent traction. As spring approached during my second year, the weather was just starting to turn nice and the temperature would occasionally hit the mid-60s (a heat wave in that part of the country).

One Friday in April, after a week of classes, the weather was uncharacteristically gorgeous. A friend and I decided to go downtown and visit one of the local pubs.

We met up with several other students from our dorm and, after being there for about two hours, I decided it was time to head back to the dorm.

Just after loading up my VW with six other friends, I saw my roommate who also asked for a ride back. When he saw that the car was packed, he said "no problem, I'll just sit on the hood" and he jumped on.

I thought he was kidding so I started to drive away. When he made no effort to get off, I pulled onto the road knowing he would quickly yell for me to let him get off.

Keeping in mind that my roommate was 6'6" and weighed about 240 pounds, this must have been quite a sight and I could barely see out the front windshield.

After I drove for about a quarter of a mile, we were passed by a local policeman going the other way who quickly pulled me over and cited us. Here is how the local paper described it:

Car Clinging Nets Arrest

Canton - Village police arrested two Canton students in connection with "joy riding" incident on Main Street Friday afternoon. Michael Kirk, 18, Plattsburgh, was charged with clinging to a vehicle (riding on the hood of a compact car full of students), and the driver of the vehicle, Daniel J. Arena, 18, Rome, was charged with permitting clinging and obstructed vision.

(Note: The obstructed vision charge was for a cracked windshield.)

Dan Arena

HOLD THE ANCHOVIES

One particular evening from my adolescence rates high in the scrapbooks. It involved a 16-year-old driver (me), and a 1969 Bug painted an obnoxious neon orange with a hint of candy apple red.

You knew you were really cool when your car had a custom leather steering wheel approximately eight inches in diameter, very hip driving lights, black spoiler, custom padded black velour panels on the doors, large and cheap speakers built into the cubby hole in the back, and a 500-watt power booster duct tape fitted into the cardboard glove box! And just below the glove box: a black tachometer with a big red dial that you could set for redline. Of course, it had mags. And to top it off, a very loud exhaust system. This muffler had a low, distinct roar. There was nothing wimpy about it. We're talking the roar in second and third gear that Mom and Dad could hear 10 blocks away. The roar that the entire side of the high school would recognize at 8:27 a.m. every weekday as I careened into the parking lot and bolted into the building to beat the 8:30 a.m. home room bell. Ah, the memories. This Bug had it all.

Occasionally, the stereo's power booster would heat up more than normal and catch the cardboard glove box on fire. (Hey, I think I got it for $9.99 at the weekly car stereo liquidation). Fortunately, this only occurred when the car was driving. I would have hated to be sitting in algebra class, staring out the window and seeing flames coming out the hood of my Bug! "Uh, can I be excused for a minute? My Bug is on fire!"

Two features completed this "classic". First, custom drilled holes in the floorboard, just around the battery under the back seat. You see, the car leaked when it rained. Dad and I could never find where it came from, we just knew that an inch or two of standing water didn't make for a haven of electrical safety when the car battery was sitting in it. So, we took the logical route and said "To hell with it. We can't keep water from coming in, so we might as well let it flow to the back and exit." Father and son engineering at its finest!

Now the last feature of my Bug is where this one particular night ranks highest in my annals of teenage history. My best friend, Ken, (or "Rockhead," as most called him) was manager of the local carry-out and pizza store. Every night, after I would get off work from my busboy job, I would stop by his pizza place and drink beer in the back kitchen. This particular evening I think the beer was exceptionally strong. Rockhead got the bright idea that we would take a vat of pizza grease and pour it over the paved parking lot next door. The lot had a particularly short and steep section to it. The reasoning was this would make for nice donuts and tire spinning in the Bug. That one additional custom feature of my Bug "made" this evening: Bald radials. My Dad had been after me for months to replace the tires. Rockhead and I had just discovered the reason for holding out. Pizza grease and bald tires make a superb replacement for lack of torque and power!

Well, after two or three hours of burning tires and pizza grease and about 3,000 donuts, it was time to go home. The stench of burning rubber and pizza grease was indescribable. Driving 100 feet out of the lot, it became apparent that the bald tires and pizza grease had fused. Every little touch on the gas pedal would send the Bug into an uncontrollable slide that, when counteracted, would produce a full 360-degree spin. We could actually drive around town and execute precision "fishtails" and "donuts" on command! This novel idea took us into the wee hours until steel threads began poking out of the radials.

The following Saturday, the tire store couldn't understand how the rear tires on a Bug could be worn straight through to the steel belts! Oh, to be young and driving an orange Bug!

Brent Flory

WATER BUGS

It was the spring of 1966, a very damp year for Wade Park, Minnesota. We had city-wide flooding. After observing two Red Cross rescue boats helping stranded residents off their roofs, I decided to put my '66 blue Beetle into the same flood waters. Yes, it was as watertight as the sales brochure promised, plus it was faster than the rescue boats. The next day I took it to my delivering dealer and complained about the wet rear carpet, which he proceeded to clean and dry for me at no charge. He couldn't find a leak in the door seals. I guess I shouldn't have tried reverse because when I did the heater ducts ran like fire hydrants in all that water!

Over the next year I had several chances to test my "VW boating theory".

One was in the gulf off Padre Island, Texas, another was off Diamond Head in Hawaii. The Pacific experience ended my VW boating days. At that time, being from Minnesota, I didn't understand tides and undertow and off went the rental agency's Beetle into the sea and surf. Luckily, three swimmers came to my rescue and pulled me and my car back onto the safety of the shore. It would have been hard to explain to the car rental company.

Now I live on the gulf and have two real boats. But you can't drive them home from the beach after a day's fun in the water. I sure miss my blue VW boat with the whitewall tires.

A. Jay Trepanier

FOLLOWING THE FOLLOWER

"I've Decided to Follow Jesus", is what the back of his truck said. It was an old, blue Ford pickup with that statement hand-painted in red on the tailgate. It was the summer of 1995. I was going into Denver on I-25 south, which had only one lane open because of construction. I couldn't pass. I could only stare at the declaration on my fellow traveler's tailgate and muse about its meaning — and the divine vehicle that must be ahead of it.

"I wonder what kind of car Jesus would drive? Would it use real gas? I wonder what state He got His license in? Would a cop really pull Jesus over? And if he did, would the cop give Him a ticket? I wonder what He's doing in Denver? I wonder if He has personalized license plates?" All of these thoughts ran through my mind. No disrespect was intended; I figured He would approve of my speculation about His place in my day-to-day life.

We made our way through the construction site, and the Interstate opened up to three lanes.

"Finally I can pass this truck and catch a glimpse of Jesus," I thought. "Should I wave to Him? Should I invite Him to lunch?"

We passed the truck. Nothing. Nothing special anyway. I didn't see the black, stretch limousine that I expected to see.

"Of course", I thought. "Jesus is humble. He must be in that old, brown Toyota Corolla up there." I sped up to catch the run-down car. Nothing! Nothing even close. In the Corolla was a woman with pink foam curlers in her hair, smoking a cigarette.

The next day walking down 16th street I found it. I found who the guy in the pick-up truck must have been following. It was parked on the side of the road right in front of the Denver public library. A green Volkswagen Bug. The only reason I knew it was Jesus' Volkswagen was because there was a sticker in the rear window of His face.

"What a perfect place for Jesus," I thought. "At the library. That's where you can learn about anything. Except He already knows everything. Maybe He just likes the quiet," I thought.

I kept walking down the street. I wanted to talk to Him but I didn't want to bother Him while he was at the library. He probably just wanted to be alone for a while. To get away from the people who were following Him in his Bug on the Interstate.

"I wonder what happened to the guy in the pickup. Did he take the wrong turn-off? Couldn't his pickup truck keep up with Jesus' green Volkswagen?" And why a VW? Because it's "the people's car?" These thoughts plagued my mind as I whistled, and continued to walk down the street. Some mysteries are supposed to remain that way.

Tyler LaFon

TIME TRAVEL

It was May of 1997, nearly a year before VW's reintroduced version of the Beetle would be available to the public. I received a frantic phone call from a friend claiming that he had just spotted four of the prototypes on Highway 285 heading south somewhere around Como, Colorado. I was very excited because this meant that they were heading in my direction and would be driving through in about 15 minutes.

I scrambled out the door mumbling something to my employees about "important research" and jumped into my faithful '66 Beetle. I pulled my camera from the glove box and drove to an intersection to wait. This was going to be big. The renaissance of the Bug had been in the making for a while but no one had actually seen one on the road yet.

Like clockwork the four prototypes, then known as "Concept 1's", passed right before my eyes: two red, one white, and one black, at about 60 mph. I was thrilled at the sight. I waved as they sped by and the drivers stared at my '66 like it was some ancient classic relic to the VW world. I was the past. They were the future.

I pulled out onto the highway and worked to accelerate up to their cruising speed. The Concept 1's obviously intended to cover some serious ground. Before long, they were averaging close to 80 mph and my '66 was barely able to keep up.

We continued this pace for about 45 miles until thankfully in the middle of nowhere they decided to pull over on the side of the road to have lunch. I pulled in behind the convoy of Concepts and started taking pictures.

Not a word of English was spoken as I approached. The drivers all were German and very interested in my camera. They managed to convey that they were not too pleased with me taking pictures of them or the cars.

Having gotten a few good keepsake pictures, I didn't want to ruin the moment, so I jumped in my vintage Beetle and started the trip back to work. VW has started its Bug-era trip back, too. Only time will tell where theirs will end with the new Beetle. The story is about to begin again.

Scott Atchison

EPILOGUE

Although the era that inspired "Bug Tales" has ended, a new one may be beginning.

Following years of calls and letters from people just like the ones who contributed to this book, Volkswagen responded. At a glitzy Detroit event in early 1998 we saw a car that respects its heritage but embraces the future.

Does it replace the Bug?

"No, we are not bringing the Beetle back," VW executive Dr. Jens Neumann said. "We bring you the new Beetle — a very modern car that we all seem to have known for a long time; an evolutionary work of art that has become dear to our hearts long before we could touch it for the first time."

Or, as VW Chairman Dr. Ferdinand Piech said: "The new Beetle cannot deny its origin and the magic of its shape."

We don't know if it will be the bestseller the original was. One thing's for sure, though. It's got a tough act to follow.

Peace, love and Bugs!

INDEX

Adolph, 181
Aircraft, 7
Agan, Jim, 147
Alamo, 88
Andrews, Dave, 109
Andrews, Gemma, 45
Angels, 55, 63
Annie, 47
Arena, Dan, 226
Ashford, Ken, 156
Atchison, Scott, 233
Aunt Hazel, 178
Badger, Donna, 126
Barnett, Cindy, 164
Bass, 15
Bayles, Donna and Rick, 30
Beam, Elizabeth Ditto, 16
Bees, 185, 197
Benny, 176
Berckman, Bill, 123
Bertie, 45
Bethlehem, 91
Biedinger, Dick, 160, 215
Bill collector, 71
Brazil, 159
Brown, Steve, 169
Bugg, Mr., 164
Butler, Mel and Rosalie, 209
Byler, Josh, 143
Calimanzi, 134
Camping, 42, 75, 77
Canary, Christopher, 174

Cancer, 45
Cantinieri, Joe, 168
Carnahan, Suzanne, 14
Case, Bob, 176
Catherine, 18
Christmas, 91, 152, 207
Church, 207
Cigarette lighter, 127
Circus, 203
Concept 1's, 233
Cooler, 60
Cows, 187, 197
Cream Puff, 22
Dachshund, 199
Decker, Bev and Gene, 144
Dempster, H. Scott, 158
Eckerle, Jeff, 101
Elephant, 203
Engine parts, 210
Estate sale, 32
Fisk, Mark C., 190
Fitzpatrick, W.W., 22
Floating, 126, 230
Flory, Brent, 228
Fortenbery, Jeff, 105
Freel, Chris, 194
Friedman, Jim, 86
Gerbil, 192
Godby, Jeff, 151
Golden, Bella and Richard, 77
Gorilla suit, 65

Gra', 65
Grace, Lois E., 67
Graybeal, James H., 166
Groovey, 30
Guidry, Penny, 60
Gulley, Benjamin Jr., 187
Hall, Douglas E., 219
Hansen, Kristin, 15
Harriet, 55
Hartman, Phyllis, 127
Heidi, 51
Henry, John S., 118
Hess, Duane, 162
Holtzknecht, Dave, 41
Honey, Dr. Edward, 107
Hooter, 30
Imhoff, Dick, 20, 93
Inspections, 215
Janson, Dennis, 136
Jesus, 231
Johnson, James B., 81
Jordan, Marcus, 75
Joyride, 162
Kaelin, Lana, 161
Keller, Terri, 111
Klebahn, Paul, 82, 112, 152
LaFon, Tyler, 231
Lard, 223
Lions, 194
Lomax, John R. Jr., 39
Louderback, Tom and Carolyn, 179
Ludwig, Tanja, 35

Marijuana, 16
McKinney, Sarah, 63
Meiner, Randy, 124
Morocco, 93
Moths, 190
Motorcycles, 124
Motor Trend, 10
Murphy, Kevin, 51
Narus, Don, 3
Navy, 7, 210
Nelson, Taylor, 18
Old Beetle Finder, 22
Overbeck, Stephen F., 210
Packing peanuts, 140
Parker, Marianne Diehl, 178
Patton, Michael C., 207
Pisani, Paula, 55
Pizza grease, 229
Pony, 185
Pottery, 128
Price, Keith, 32
Prison, 174
Prom night, 18
Ramis, Harold, 116
Rawlins, Patti, 172
Red Menace, 26
Reverse, 14
Robbins, Sabin, 62
Robin, 201
Rockhead, 228
Roth, Rev. John, 185
Rubber band, 104
Schmidbauer, Bill, 91
Schryver, Margaret, 198

Schulz, Kirk and Pam, 192
Seats, 123, 219
Shirk, Dave, 201
Shoestrings, 50
Simpson, Brenda, 199
Singler, Joe, 96
Sister Clove, 65
Smith, Steffi, 159
Soccer field, 77
Sondahl, Brad, 128
Stulz, Mary Ann Geiman, 216
Swimming pool, 101
Szturm, Jill, 170
Thiemann, George, 223
Thier, Cooki, 59
Third gear, 16
Throttle cable, 112
Topas, 82
Tope, William G., 203
Trepanier, A. Jay, 230
Tubing, 107
Tune, C. Van, 10
Tuohy, Jim, 104
Turpin, Mark, 134
Udell, Rochelle, 133
Underwear, 96
Van Der Woude, William G., 12
Vern, 67
Vodka, 105
Waller, Robert, 47
West, Kathy, 164
Wilson, Bruce L., 71

Winters, Dave, 48
Woolley, Bryan, 26
Worrall, Andrew, 138
Zampino, Sherry, 181

Paul Klebahn

Paul Klebahn's fascination with all things automotive — but particularly Volkswagens — is, quite literally, a lifelong one. The co-author of Bug Tales was taken home from the hospital in one by his parents in 1964 and his father adapted the back seat area of a Bug into a makeshift playpen so Paul could travel with him more comfortably. Many of his earliest childhood memories revolve around traveling in his father's Bug.

Over the years Paul restored many VWs and Porsches, as his fascination with air-cooled engines grew. Meanwhile, he earned degrees in business administration and psychology, and worked as sales and marketing manager for several Cincinnati-area companies.

Through his business and social contacts, he'd heard many peoples' anecdotes about their VWs. Encouraged by the volume and variety of those anecdotes he embarked upon "Bug Tales."

Gabriella Jacobs

Gabriella Jacobs has been a professional writer and editor for over 20 years. Her career began as a high school correspondent for her hometown daily newspaper, and continued. She later worked there as a reporter while earning a degree in mass communication, tuition money for that degree, and the downpayment on a robin's-egg-blue VW.

Later she held a variety of editorial positions at both one of the smallest and one of the largest daily newspapers in Indiana, worked as an editor/proofreader for a legal publishing company in Ohio, was copy editor of a weekly business journal and then editor of a biweekly one. Her freelance writing has appeared in numerous newspapers and magazines.

She is currently the editor of a national engineering organization's technical journal and communications specialist for the organization's many projects. Her VW was retired in the early 1980s, when a mechanic declared that she had "driven the life out of it."

TELL US YOUR TALE!
Why?

FUN NoSTaLgia cure boredom   Embarrass your family

Cheap ego boost   Impress your friends

Fame   NOTORIETY   Expand your book collection?   Memories
       THERAPY   ENHANCE YOUR WARDROBE?
                 Win bets with friends that you're in a book

What ever your reasons, ours is for the fun of it. Like many people, we love VW's and the great times We've had in them. We feel a quality series of books is the best way to share all of our experiences and our love for our favorite cars with the world.

If your story is included in one of the books, you'll receive a "Hey, I'm in Bug Tales" t-shirt and a free copy of that edition of the book upon its release.

How To Submit Stories

E-mail: **Bugtales@aol.com**
Snail Mail: Bug Tales
                     P.O. Box 76272
                 Highland Heights, KY 41076
                         USA
Call   (513) 956-7459
Fax: (606) 442-7110

Unfortunately, not all stories can be included. If we feel your story may be used in one of the books, you will be sent a permission form allowing us to use your name and edit the story as needed. Contributors will also have the option of "anonymous" if they do not wish to have their name appear in the series. Sorry, no stories will be included with out the contributor's signature or the signature of a legal guardian on our permission form.

Thank you and see you on the road!